Notes fi
End of History

Notes from the End of History

A Memoir of the Left in Wales

PHILIP BOUNDS

MERLIN PRESS

First published in 2014 by
The Merlin Press
99B Wallis Road
London
E9 5LN

www.merlinpress.co.uk

ISBN. 978-0-85036-611-2

Printed in the UK by Imprint Digital, Exeter

CONTENTS

For Daisy, with love and admiration

Everyone who studies Marx, it is said, feels compelled to write a book about the experience.
David Harvey, *The Limits to Capital*

Undoubtedly, one of the greatest problems which each of us has to solve in the realm of practice, is that of accepting the necessity to maintain, in the midst of the intransigence which comes from steadfast beliefs, a critical spirit towards these same beliefs and a respect for the belief that differs.
Victor Serge, *Memoirs of a Revolutionary*

And yet, as I drove home from my interview with the leader, I had to realize that a liberal, incurably, was what I was. Whatever I might argue, I was more profoundly attached to liberal concepts of freedom – freedom of speech and of the press, academic freedom, independent judgement and independent judges – than I was to the idea of a disciplined party mobilizing all the forces of society for the creation of a social order guaranteeing more real freedom for all instead of just for a few. The revolutionary idea both impressed me and struck me as more *immediately* relevant for most of humanity than were the liberal concepts. But it was the liberal concepts and their long-term importance – though not the name of liberal – that held my allegiance.
Conor Cruise O'Brien, *Writers and Politics*

[It is possible to] … carry ourselves back in thought to those moments of our life when we made some serious decision, moments unique of their kind, which will never be repeated – any more than the past phases in the history of a nation will ever come back again.
Henri Bergson, *Time and Free Will*

Of course it is true in many cases, and it may be true in all cases, that revolutionary activity is the result of personal maladjustment ... But after all, this does not invalidate the Socialist case ... History has to move in a certain direction, even if it has to be pushed that way by neurotics.
George Orwell, *Arthur Koestler*

PREFACE

In the last few weeks of 1989, when the Berlin Wall was breached and the socialist regimes in Eastern Europe were toppled, it was widely believed that Marxists would be all but extinct by the year 2000. This belief was powerfully reinforced by the ignominious collapse of the Soviet Union in 1991. Humanity had apparently arrived at the 'end of history' (a phrase popularised by the political theorist Francis Fukuyama) and any thought of finding an alternative to capitalism would have to be abandoned. It has now become clear that these predictions were wide of the mark. The number of people calling themselves Marxists has certainly gone down over the last twenty years, but the socialist and communist movements still exist and appear to be experiencing a modest renaissance. Times have changed and the strengths of the free market no longer seem quite so self-evident. Indeed, in the wake of the sudden implosion of the international financial system in the autumn of 2008, it has become fashionable to argue that capitalism's survival can no longer be taken for granted. History has returned with a vengeance.

Why did so many people retain their faith in Marxism after the collapse of 'actually existing socialism'? Most of them would say that Marxism is true and that its truth is not compromised by the disappearance of a few lousy governments. I happen to agree with them about this, but the purpose of this memoir of life on the left is not to weigh up the pros and cons of a particular political doctrine. My focus is on another explanation for the survival of Marxism, one which many of its adherents seem too embarrassed to acknowledge – the fact that Marxism (like Christianity or Islam before it) played a central role in shaping people's sense of who they were. The thousands of malcontents who signed up to communist or Trotskyist parties were never merely engaged in a struggle for political progress. They were also placing a bet on the possibility of personal redemption. Marxism worked on their minds and their bodies like a piece of great art, reaching into the deepest recesses of their souls and transforming them into different (and usually better) people than they had been before. To those who were most immersed in it – to those whose every response was shaped by it – the thought of abandoning socialist politics was tantamount to tearing up the sinews of selfhood and starting again from scratch. It was all too much to bear.

Notes from the End of History records the impact of Marxism on the mind of an individual. It tries to show how the development of a particular sensibility was bound up with broader developments in politics, culture and thought. In this sense the book is as much a work of social history as a memoir. Its author has never been influential in national politics nor even in the fringe organisations to which he has belonged. None of that matters. The point about Marxism was that it affected its minnows as deeply as its sharks, intruding a sense of the extraordinary into even the most commonplace lives. It is no accident that most of the events I describe took place in Wales's second city but could have occurred anywhere.

Memoirs do not usually provide an unimpeachable record of the past. This one is no exception. Its relationship with my personal history is not an entirely faithful one. Some of the people who appear in it are composites, fusing the traits of separate individuals into a single character. Many of its scenes conflate things that occurred at different times and different places. Nevertheless, the story it tells is as true as it needs to be. Like most books about being young, it regularly evokes epiphanies – moments when one's angle of vision suddenly changes and life is transformed forever. I do not imagine for a moment that my life is of interest to anyone other than myself. I have written about my experiences because I believe they shed some light on the wider culture of the left. All names, except those of public figures, have been changed.

INTRODUCTION
Hitting the Streets

Every Saturday evening I receive an e-mail circular from a voluble Yorkshireman called Alasdair. Written in a species of bureaucratese and littered with errors of punctuation, it reports on that day's efforts by members of the Communist Party in Wales to campaign in a local town or city. In his capacity as Welsh Secretary of the Party, Alasdair thanks the handful of people who turned out in Cardiff, Deeside or Pontypridd to distribute leaflets and spread the word. His tone is often reproachful and celebratory at the same time. Scolding those of us who failed to make an appearance ('Comrades need to reconsider their level of commitment to Party activities'), he does his best to portray tiny advances as major victories. Seven copies of the *Morning Star* were sold, or so he tells us. Two students expressed an interest in attending the next branch meeting in Cardiff. A pensioner donated 50p and reminisced about the miners' strike of 1972.

I confess that I have only gone campaigning on a few occasions since I turned forty in 2007. One day in particular sticks in my mind. Temporarily enthused by the arrival of a new year, I drove the sixty or so miles from Swansea to Cardiff on a freezing Saturday in January and joined seven other comrades for a couple of hours of 'street activity'. Along for the ride was my partner Jasmine, who wisely tends to eschew politics (the result of her upbringing in North-East India) but cautiously respects anyone who calls himself a Marxist. Our first task was to set up a trestle table at the foot of the statue of Aneurin Bevan on Queen Street. After covering it with a red flag and taping 'Defend the NHS' posters to its front, we piled it high with pamphlets, CDs and books. Then we spread out and tried to foist our leaflets on the passers-by.

I had forgotten how ghastly this sort of thing could be. Huddling close to Jasmine and making weak jokes about the apathy of the public, I had to force myself to walk up to people and ask them to take a leaflet. My strike rate was pitifully low. Nearly everyone under thirty either ignored me or said 'no thanks', save for a genial young man with a learning disorder who told me all about his pet snake. The middle-aged were generally more receptive, though I noticed that no one actually read a leaflet before folding it in half and consigning it to a pocket. As ever, our only real success was with the old.

'So you're *communists*, are you?' The speaker was a woman in her eighties who had just seen the hammer and sickle emblazoned on our posters. Sprightly, bursting with opinions and well-dressed in a respectable tweed coat, she presented a very recognisable type. I had a fair idea of what was coming. She reached into her handbag and pulled out a sheaf of small booklets, most of them published by a nonconformist sect whose apocalyptic leanings are a matter of legend. She gave a booklet each to Jasmine and me and then paused for a moment as our eyes alighted on the question that served as a title: 'Are You Wasting Your Time?'

'I'm a Christian', she explained. 'I believe that we all have to make our peace with God before the Day of Judgement.' I was tempted to say 'Listen, love – I'm afraid I'm past saving' but politeness got the better of me. Instead I smiled as charmingly as I could and listened to her point of view. She pursued what I'm tempted to call a Gramscian strategy, seeking to meet us half-way in order to inflect our thoughts in the direction of Christ. 'I can quite understand what communists like you are trying to do', she said. 'You believe in decency and I respect that. Some of your policies I agree with. For example, I thoroughly approve of imprisoning homosexuals and drug addicts. Say what you like about the Soviet Union but it always ensured that its citizens led modest and responsible lives.'

The old lady's speech produced a familiar stab of dismay just above my left eye. It seemed extraordinary that someone could have misunderstood us so completely. Should I interrupt her and try to put her straight? Or should I just let her carry on? I winced at the thought of telling her that the excesses of the Soviet Union had nothing to do with communism. I knew she wouldn't take it well when I told her that people like me believed in individual liberty – that we *defended* the rights of gays, lesbians and all the other people she wanted to send to prison. But in the end I didn't have to.

The weather saved me. A violent gust of wind lurched across Queen Street and brought the most extraordinary hailstorm in its wake. My Christian interlocutor disappeared. Seven communists and an Indian fellow traveller rushed to the trestle table and pulled it under the awning of a shop. To prevent things blowing away we rested our hands on our cargo of merchandise and waited for the winds to die down. Cardiff turned white in a matter of seconds. A thick layer of hail settled on the roads, the pavements and the expanse of grass outside the castle. The sky took on that curiously anaemic look that puts one in mind of the darkest recesses of Russia. I joked that the council must have known we were communists and laid on Siberian weather for our benefit. Jasmine was more succinct: 'It's beautiful', she said.

We had to wait about ten minutes before we could pull the table back into the street and resume our leafleting. For a few moments I felt a rumbling of unease in my Marxist-Leninist soul. My chat with the elderly Christian had unsettled me. Her misunderstandings about Marxism and the Soviet Union were neither here nor there – I'd heard that sort of thing nearly every day for twenty-five years. What really rattled me was the fact that she'd called me a communist. Suddenly I felt beleaguered by a terrible lack of sophistication. I wanted to chase after my Christian friend and tell her that no one was really a communist anymore, that none of us believed that the millennium would ever arrive or that the expropriators would ever be expropriated. I wanted to tell her that my membership of the Party was *elegiac* – a sort of perverse middle-aged tribute to a movement that had bedazzled me in my youth, stuffed my ignorant head with a simulacrum of learning and then collapsed under the weight of its own ambitions. Instead I fell to brooding.

Why did I react so badly to being called a communist? Why had I suddenly wanted to disavow all the beliefs I was supposedly trying to promote? I suppose it was partly a matter of narcissism: I didn't want the trajectory of my life misrepresented by a stranger who knew nothing about it. It was clear from the way she spoke to me that the old woman had marked me down as one of life's true believers. She obviously regarded me as the sort of person who embraces a few crude ideas as a thoughtless young man and clings to them dogmatically for the rest of his life. When she spoke about the need for repentance and the entry of the righteous into the Kingdom of Heaven, she gave the distinct impression that she thought I'd never heard of Christianity before. The thought that I'd ever engaged with other people's ideas or questioned the rectitude of my own was clearly beyond her. To her I was just another pitiful heathen, trapped in a demonic ideology by my refusal to hear what more enlightened folk had to say.

The cheek of it all! As I stood there waiting for the hail to end, I grimaced self-indulgently at the thought of all the little agonies which membership of the communist movement had brought me. My relationship with Marxism had been anything but easy. I first came across it as a boy of fifteen, desperate in the tumultuous world of the early 1980s to find something that would mark me out from my more successful peers. Thrilled by its promise of a society in which even the lowliest person might flourish, I had no idea that the demands it made on its adherents were often too arduous to be borne. In those early days my Marxism was purely a matter of slogans, wide-eyed utopianism and adolescent bumptiousness. I thought it the height of sophistication to shout 'Workers of the world, unite!'

at a passing police car or paint a red star on a toilet wall. It was only when I began to study it seriously, a couple of months after my seventeenth birthday, that I began to realise what a stern taskmaster it could be. My first encounter with Marxist theory was at once the most liberating and the most terrifying experience of my life. The realisation that Marx had provided a theory of *everything* – that he purported to explain the whole of human history from the emergence of *Homo sapiens* to the terminal crises of industrial capitalism – excited me more profoundly than anything before or since. At the same time it filled me with anxieties that have never gone away. I had been a miserable failure at school and my ignorance was prodigious. How dare I suppose that the labyrinthine complexities of history could ever be understood by a dunderhead like me?

At the age of eighteen I went to university and parlayed my scanty knowledge of Marxism into a fair amount of academic success. Then came the fall. Exhausted from trying to cram too much knowledge into too small a cranium – reduced to a state of nervous collapse by Lenin's injunction that communists should 'Study! Study! Study!' – I succumbed to a bout of ill-health whose effects lasted for years. For nearly a decade I wrestled with a species of religious mania which left me all but incapable of functioning; Marxism had laid me low. My growing distance from the Communist Party was powerfully reinforced by the cataclysmic political reversals of the age. The onward march of Thatcherism pointed to a future in which the market would go unchallenged. The collapse of the socialist countries seemed to confirm what every right-wing killjoy had ever said about them. Something like two years elapsed between the overthrow of the Stalinist states in Eastern Europe and the Soviet Union's last bow. In that time my commitment to the cause dwindled almost to nothing. As soon as the USSR was gone I began to call myself a 'lapsed Marxist' and assumed that my days of revolutionary fervour were behind me. I was hollowed out by political grief.

The very fact that I was there in Cardiff, thrusting poorly produced leaflets into the hands of an indifferent public, showed that my estrangement from Marxism had not lasted. In the end I had recovered my health and returned to the Party, unwilling to abandon the dream of a better society and the sense of meaning that went with it. I knew perfectly well that the intensities of my adolescence could never be recaptured, but after everything the world and I had been through – the wars, the depressions, the breakdowns – I decided that muted idealism was much to be preferred to sophisticated despair. Every day I mustered what faith I could in the face of gnawing doubts about the wisdom of what I was doing. A true believer I most certainly was not.

The second hour of campaigning went more quickly than the first. After it was over and the people from the Cardiff Branch were carrying the trestle table back to the car, Jasmine and I spent a couple of minutes looking at the statue of Bevan and chatting about the man it represented. I told her who Bevan was and explained that few men had made a bigger contribution to the civilising of Britain. She heard me out politely and spoke about the desperate need for socialised health care in India: 'It's too bad that you people exported the free market but not socialism', she observed. I shot her a rueful grin and we headed off to the car park, anxious to get out of the cold and back to Swansea as soon as possible. The mere act of talking about Bevan had inflamed my anxieties about the past. In his day the young men of Wales joined the Labour Movement in their early teens and remained passionately committed to it until the end of their lives. My record of agonised ambivalence would probably have appalled them. As we drove past the walls of Cardiff Castle on our way out to the motorway, I began to realise that the old lady's question would have to be answered after all.

Had I been wasting my time?

CHAPTER 1
Out of my Class

The first thing to do is to dispel any impression of virtue. One anecdote should do the trick. In my first year at university I ate far too many takeaway meals from Kentucky Fried Chicken. One evening in early December, shortly after leaving the pub, I stood in line with a couple of friends and prepared to place my order. In front of me in the queue was a woman in her twenties who gave off what my Philosophy tutor liked to call 'deeply contradictory signals'. She had clearly been out for the evening and had done her best to look glamorous. Her burgundy dress was sleeveless, short and appeared to be made from velvet. A chiffon scarf was thrown insouciantly over her shoulder and her high-heeled shoes were eye-catching without being ostentatious. Judged by her outfit alone she could have been a nurse, a teacher or an estate agent. The rest of her was a study in council-estate brutalism. Her lank, medium-length hair had been bleached to within an inch of its life, though very dark roots were beginning to show along her centre parting. Her body was bone-revealingly thin (not that mine was much better) and hinted at minute-to-minute unhappiness rather than anorexia or illness. Her complexion was ashen and the large pores on her cheeks seemed to be widening into premature wrinkles. It was almost as if her DNA had rebelled against the pressure of keeping up appearances, endowing her with a look that said 'Don't believe the dress! I'm dirt poor and I defy you to do anything about it!'

And then there was the temper. She ordered the cheapest meal on the menu and paid with a pound coin. When the waitress failed to give her any change, she said 'I thought the meal cost ninety-nine pence.' 'That's right', replied the waitress. 'So where's my fucking penny, then?' she retorted. Her voice was threatening enough to reduce a queue of bibulous students to silence. As she took her meal and stalked out, holding her penny in the palm of her left hand with the ends of her bony fingers, none of us had the nerve to meet her gaze.

On the walk back to campus I made some disapproving noises. I told my friend Colin, a scrupulously polite student of Computer Science, that the woman in KFC had fussed grotesquely over nothing. What was the point of being so rude for the sake of a lousy penny? His response was witheringly incisive. 'The problem with you', he observed, 'is that you don't understand poverty. Or rather – you understand it intellectually but you've never felt it on your pulses. It's all very well making an impression at the student bar with your revolutionary slogans, but I'd have more respect for you if you actually thought about the working class occasionally.' I suppose I should have been outraged. Since arriving at university I had played up my membership of the Communist Party for all it was worth. Surrounded by confident students from the South of England whose maturity greatly exceeded my own, I had set myself up as the doughty tribune of the poor – principled, instinctively egalitarian, contemptuous of Thatcherism and all its consumerist fripperies. Colin's accusations struck at the very heart of my identity. In effect he was telling me that my politics were grossly insincere and that I was little better than a fraud. Yet his remark about my making an impression at the student bar filled me with delight. After a lifetime of fading tediously into the background – never being singled out or praised or mentioned in dispatches for *anything* – I at last had reason to hope that one or two people were sitting up and taking notice. It was the first sign that possibly – just possibly – my project of self-transformation was beginning to work.

———

The moral of this sordid little story is clear. My teenage conversion to Marxism had very little to do with sympathy for the poor. I was not one of those ardent adolescents whose blood froze at the site of squalid high-rise flats, undernourished children and lengthening dole queues. When I decided at the age of fifteen years and three months that I was going to become a communist, I didn't even try to convince myself that compassion or anger at injustice were the motivating factors. I knew perfectly well that I was playing for higher stakes than that. What I was really looking for was something that could save me from myself.

I attended my first meeting of a Marxist organisation in the spring of 1982. There are several photos of me from just before this time, all of them taken in my aunt's house in the South Wales valleys. The human material they depict is scarcely very distinguished. I look like a waif. My appearance is not that of a young man but of an overgrown boy – one whose diffident brown eyes, emaciated body and ashen complexion betray no great desire to leave the world of childhood behind. At a time when my more fashionable contemporaries are trying to look like Paul Weller, Simon le Bon or some other dandified pop star, I'm decked out in clothes of a quite unimaginable drabness. My navy jeans are absurdly baggy and concertina above my black trainers. My v-necked sweatshirt is brown (naturally), slightly threadbare and worn over a cheap red t-shirt. And the hair! Regularly chopped but clearly never styled, it reaches down in unlayered brown straggles to the top of my eyebrows and the bottom of my ears. This is a boy who has never turned a head in his life, except in derision.

When a friend of mine saw these photographs nearly twenty years after they were taken, she immediately put her scanty knowledge of psychology to work and diagnosed Asperger's Syndrome. 'Just look at you', she said. 'You're occupying space but somehow you're not there.' She probably had a point. Looking as objectively as I can at that utterly characterless boy, I realise that he's not even on speaking terms with the world in which he lives. He knows nothing. The most basic facts about the most basic things are entirely unfamiliar to him. He spends most of his time sequestered in his own head, utterly indifferent to the efforts of his relatives, his teachers and his not-very-numerous friends to equip him with the skills he needs to stay alive. But his ignorance is also his strength. Beneath that shambolic exterior the soul of a hapless dreamer is beginning to stir. Too naive to realise that life has a brisk way with fantasists, he cherishes the thought that his failure to fit in is somehow a portent of an unusual future. His intuition tells him that the fates are about to show their hand. Perhaps his destiny is to escape the crippling burden of normality which bourgeois civilisation imposes on everyone else. Standing there while his doting aunt takes his photo – cruelly aware that she is one of the few people who takes him seriously – he is biding his time and waiting for something to happen.

Like most adolescents who console themselves with thoughts of their own uniqueness, I was as typical as a minor character in an eighteenth-century novel. If I chose to turn away from the world, it was only because its conflicting trends had shaped me so faithfully in their own image. In no way were the dilemmas I faced unusual. They were those of a smallish fraction of an insecure class at a bewildering moment of historical transition. I'll try and explain. Sometime in the late 1940s, in the grim days of demob suits, boiled cabbage and sterling crises, my parents had become the first people in their respective families to go to university. The starchy dons of Aberystwyth and Cardiff turned them into exemplary citizens of the new Wales, plying useful trades in education and science. Thousands of their compatriots had taken a similar route at about the same time, starting out in humble (though not necessarily working-class) homes and rising through the professions after years of hard work in grammar schools and colleges. So mine were the problems of the second-generation middle class in an age when the borders between classes were more permeable than ever. The issue at stake was whether I could prove equal to the example I had been set. Would I sink or swim? Did the middle class have room for me or did it not? Was I to emulate my parents or was I to slip back into something less successful, less effortful, less respectable?

In no sense was I the sort of child who harnesses the middle-class pony and gallops with it. The story of my first two decades is not one of exams passed, instruments learned or debating societies addressed. Instead I had a talent for avoiding work and running away from challenges that in retrospect strikes me as almost pathological. What on earth was wrong with me? In my more self-exculpatory moments I like to put the blame on my earliest teachers. For all their pedagogical devotion, which they reminded us about at regular intervals, they were too low on the academic ladder to regard education as altogether natural. Constantly reminding us that book learning was the most important thing in the world, they unwittingly made it clear that their own academic progress had brought them no pleasure at all. The impression they gave was that studying was the curse of mankind – a soul-destroying, scarifying ordeal that could only be heroically endured but never enjoyed or taken in one's stride. To many of us it seemed that cheating was the only skill worth learning. And learn it we did. In my first year in junior school I was obliged to write a short essay every weekend. On Sunday morning my mother would put my exercise book on the dining-room table and instruct me to make a start, her eyes alive with foreboding. For ages I would sit there staring at the page, staining the paper with tears of frustration. When the essay was finally written it was always a collaborative effort, my mother's (suitably infantilised) thoughts badly expressed in my own juvenile language. If this was work, I wanted nothing of it.

My refusal to take work seriously left spaces in my head that had to be filled. Mere vacancy was never my thing. From the age of about five onwards I became a tiresome obsessive, succumbing to ludicrous passions for football, skateboarding, popular music and anything else that was low on thought and high on vulgarity. Nor was my yearning for the lowbrow simply an expression of a degraded sensibility. In truth I was in headlong retreat from the disciplined virtues of middle-class life. The work ethic was not for me. What I wanted was an existence from which all effort had been expunged, a sort of utopia of the solar plexus in which the intellect slumbered but the senses were always sharp, the emotions always deep and the imagination always vivid. I wanted to be but not to do. I sometimes joked that my role model was the family cat, moving elegantly between sleep, food and play in a haze of befurred indulgence.

It was in this context that I began to entertain shallow fantasies about the dispossessed. In the two or three years before my encounter with Marxism, I grew used to refracting the existence of classes through the prism of my own yearnings. I had already established that the life of the middle classes was a horribly effortful one, endlessly bound up with anxiety about status, achievement and rank. It seemed logical to suppose that working-class people had liberated themselves from these things. At a time when the media peddled daily caricatures of crazily obstructive shop stewards, I thrilled to the sense that the workers were ingeniously and shamelessly committed to swinging the lead. Rolled cigarettes, dirty jokes, football matches, sex in alleyways, clocking off early and parading in the streets – these were the things that the workers lived for, or so the iconography of the day assured me. Taking these assumptions even further, I naturally supposed that the most liberated people of all were those at the very bottom – tramps, drunkards, the jobless and the insane. Although I could never quite see myself living on the streets, I took it for granted that personal fulfilment was inversely proportional to status. Somehow it seemed obvious that the only people worth bothering with were those who had eschewed the bourgeois treadmill on principle. My conscientious classmates would inherit the earth but they would have so little to show for it. Life belonged elsewhere.

Perhaps I exaggerate a little. No boy of fourteen or fifteen spends too much time dreaming of downward mobility or willing himself to fail. If you had asked me in 1982 what I intended to do when I left school, I'd probably have told you that I hoped to become a teacher. Yet my nascent (and admittedly very ignorant) take on the culture of the dispossessed was by no means unusual. I may have been stupid to regard working people as lazy, irresponsible and hedonistic (actually there's no 'may' about it – the mere thought of it makes me wince today) but I'm not simply making excuses when I say that I was falling in line with a national trend. The disconcerting truth is that British culture was saturated in anti-plebeian prejudice in the years when I was growing up. The first fifteen or twenty years of my life were dominated by the spectre of an insurgent proletariat. Organised labour flexed what we used to call its 'industrial muscle' more effectively in the 1970s and 1980s than at any other time since the years before the First World War. In a great wave of militancy the unions succeeded in turning governments out of office, inflicting food shortages and power cuts and ensuring that the dead went unburied and the rubbish uncollected. In response the media did everything in its power to disseminate the myth of the feckless worker. The unions regularly hit the headlines but only ever in their role as harbingers of disruption. No self-respecting situation comedy lacked a brusque character in a donkey jacket who smoked endless cigarettes, made lewd remarks about women and demanded a hefty wage for a ten-minute day. Andy Capp bestrode the nation like a parasitic colossus. The only thing that distinguished me from most of my peers was that I regarded the workers' fecklessness as a virtue. Immured in my own apathy – sullenly indifferent to the opportunities that the welfare state had sent my way – I longed for the hour when a mighty coalition of bus drivers, caretakers and dinner ladies would shut the schools forever. Paradise was a morning in bed when I should have been in double maths.

If the media culture of my youth held the workers in low regard, its attitude towards people further down the social scale gave off a surprising whiff of populism. Manual labourers received short shrift but tramps, gypsies and vagrants were often treated with a certain romantic tenderness. Tramps in particular were seen as dignified old Fagins whose desire for personal freedom was salutary so long as it was never emulated. In my early teens my attitude towards them was practically anthropological. On Saturdays a friend and I would sometimes spend twenty minutes or so watching them while eating our lunchtime chips in Castle Gardens, a tiny oblong park sandwiched between blocks of expensive shops near Wind Street. Castle Gardens was perhaps the only place in Swansea where people from different backgrounds could stare at each other without seeming rude. Insulated from the flow of pedestrians by borders thick with hedges, railings and conifers, it was one of those dark-green urban oases where class distinctions lose their capacity to divide without ever disappearing completely. All human life was there. At any given moment it played host to mothers and children feeding the pigeons (some people called it the 'pigeon park'), disaffected adolescents swigging cider, students reading cheap paperbacks or shop workers gazing distractedly into the middle distance. But the tramps were always the most distinctive presence. There was nothing in the slightest bit contemporary about them. None of them wore the tracksuits and trainers favoured by the modern homeless. Their enormous brown greatcoats, wide-brimmed hats and patched trousers would have seemed archaic in even the dingiest charity shop. They could have been Elizabethan vagabonds denouncing the sins of enclosure or the inmates of Bedlam after a successful escape. They were not of our time.

The most interesting thing about them was the way they related to each other. There were times when they almost gave the impression of experimenting with a new scheme for reconciling the individual and the collective. Whichever area of the park they chose to occupy (the lawn in front of the conifers on the right-hand side was especially favoured), they usually sat slightly apart from each other in a state of brooding self-containment.

Each tramp spent the bulk of his time communing wordlessly with a bottle of booze, staring impassively into its neck or lifting his eyes to squint at the sun. Then suddenly there'd be a brief burst of activity. Someone would lean over to get a light for his cigarette or inquire about the time by gesturing towards the spot on his wrist where his watch would once have been. Someone else would stand up, stamp his feet and administer a shoulder rub to his female companion. All these interactions were carried out with very little being said. It was a bit like witnessing an informal welfare system in which needs were communicated solely through the power of telepathy. Indulge me in a preposterous analogy. There's a celebrated passage in the work of Adrian Stokes, that most marmoreal of art critics, in which the figures in Piero della Francesca's paintings are said to be proudly self-sufficient and utterly interdependent at one and the same time. The first time I read it I thought immediately of those curiously impressive figures in Castle Gardens.

Not that the welfare system always worked, of course. When their supplies were exhausted the tramps had to look to the wider world for fraternal assistance. On these occasions they would survey everyone else in the park, identify a likely benefactor and send across an emissary to request the price of a cup of coffee. Only once was I singled out for attention, possibly on the grounds that my extreme youth connoted woefully empty pockets. Early on a spring afternoon I was approached by one of the comparatively rare female tramps, sixty if she was a day, who caught me unawares while I was reading a paper on a bench near the fountain. Her technique was practised but not especially polished. Leaning over me and rubbing her hands together to emphasise the chill in the air, she told me that she had not eaten for two days and asked for some spare change. Her violently staccato style of speaking hurled words directly into the inner ear. Welsh oratory was not her strong suit.

I gave her fifty pence and she bestowed an extravagant blessing on me. Emboldened by her success she moved along to the next bench, where she received short shrift from an aimless looking man in a suit. An initiation of sorts was about to occur. Before I knew where I was she headed back in my direction, threw herself into my lap and started pressing my face into her bewilderingly pendulous breasts. For the first time I had to come to terms with the awesome corporeality of the down and out. My amorous *grande dame* stank of alcohol. Her musty fur coat bristled with fleas and her hair was matted with grease. Worst of all was her face, which I saw with full clarity once I'd forced her to release her grip on my head. Rubbery, stub-toothed and salivating, it was horribly latticed with raised blood vessels. I decided that my only option was to draw her attention to harsh generational realities: 'For God's sake, piss off', I told her, 'I'm young enough to be your grandson!' This seemed to touch a nerve and she staggered off back to her friends, pausing only to tell me that I hadn't 'got the *crack*.' I accepted the insult with equanimity. There were limits to my populism and losing my virginity to a tramp was definitely one of them.

Castle Gardens disappeared nearly twenty years ago when the Council replaced it with the sort of concrete thoroughfare that usually gets called 'soulless'. Shortly afterwards the character of Swansea's (and indeed the nation's) tramps began to change for the worse. At times I'm inclined to ascribe the decline to changes in government policy. The tramps of my youth behaved like lovable rogues because that's how the police and the authorities treated them. Then the asylums were emptied and the council houses were sold off and the heroin became cheaper and the people sleeping on benches increased. Soon someone decided that the 'homeless' were a threat to social order and unleashed a veritable holocaust in the process. All those genial beggars in city parks were transformed overnight into the feral 'squeegee merchants' of right-wing lore, threatening old ladies outside supermarkets and defecating noisomely in the gutters. Nevertheless, I don't regret those Saturday lunchtimes in the company of the underclass. Generations of working people had thought of the tramp as a romantic figure, and even in the early 1980s – the age of upper-class arrogance *in excelsis* – there was still a lot in the wider culture that encouraged them (and me) to do so. One example in particular sticks in my mind. At the time there was a news programme called *Nationwide* that was broadcast on weekdays by the BBC. It went out at about six o' clock and commanded the attention of millions of people who were settling down for their evening meal: I still associate its presenters with the smell of fish fingers. In 1981 it broadcast a series of films by the journalist Tony Wilkinson, who disguised himself as a tramp and used a hidden camera to record life on the London streets. The whole thing enthralled me, even though my mother (who had lived through the worst years of the 1930s and knew what poverty was all about) shivered with distaste whenever it came on.

As I recall, Wilkinson set himself up as the scourge of social injustice. He railed against the conditions in which the homeless were living, excoriated the social services for their incompetence and cursed the government for its callous indifference. Yet even at the time I remember thinking that there was something about the films that subverted their noble intentions. Whether he knew it or not, Wilkinson was no more able to control his romantic instincts than I was. He too seemed to associate the tramps with a blessed liberation from effort. Poignant scenes focused on scrofulous men falling asleep on benches or in alleyways, slowly sinking into a twilight state of complete oblivion. 'Look at these rough diamonds', the images seemed to urge. 'When did you ever sleep as well as this?' Intimations of transcendence were even inscribed in the project's structure. In the earlier films, Wilkinson visited some of the worst 'doss houses' in which the London homeless could elect to spend the night – immense, dimly lit hovels boasting excrement on the bedsheets and rats in the kitchen. But slowly the emphasis changed. In the last film of all, anxious that the stink of the streets should not fester in our nostrils for too long, Wilkinson showed us one of the few hostels in London owned by a decent man and not by a Rachmanite. Its rates were cheap, its beds were clean and its meals were tolerably nutritious. As the last scenes faded from the screen, it was hard to resist the impression that London's tramps were negotiating an upward curve towards something approaching happiness. The wretched of the earth turned out to be not so wretched after all.

Over twenty years after the films were broadcast, I was forced to think about them again in unusual circumstances. I was teaching at the local university on an undergraduate course concerned with theories of representation. The students had been asked to choose a single visual image and write an essay about it, using the various theories to which they had been introduced. One of the students came up to me after a seminar and asked for some help. He had been wandering through the library and discovered a copy of the book which Wilkinson wrote to accompany his series.[1] I had never seen it before. He was thinking of writing his essay on one of the photographs and wanted to know whether that would be acceptable. The image in question portrayed an outrageously drunk old tramp sitting on the steps of a church. He was clearly not far from blacking out and was masturbating an empty cider bottle that protruded from his groin like a prosthetic penis. I told the student that the image was fine and asked him what he was going to say about it. He told me that the photographer had done a splendid job of exposing social hypocrisy. By depicting a pathetic tramp against the backdrop of a church, he had shown how little the establishment cares about the fate of the underprivileged. I agreed with him about this but asked him to think some more. Weren't there other ways of understanding the photograph? Didn't he agree with me that there was an element of romanticism in the image? He asked me what I meant and I spoke as delicately as I could about the role of the cider bottle. This was an example of the carnivalesque, or so I tried to tell him. Far from coming across as the passive victim of poverty, the tramp was actively resisting an unjust social order by indulging in an obscenely exaggerated display of public sexuality. The student was unconvinced but wanted to keep me onside. 'That's interesting', he conceded. 'To be honest I didn't notice what the tramp was doing.'

'No', I thought to myself. 'I don't suppose you did.'

---

1 See Tony Wilkinson, *Down and Out* (London: Quartet Books, 1981).

My ambiguous class identity wasn't the only source of anxiety as I moved uncertainly through my adolescence. Issues of morality also caused me problems. Here too I was typical of at least the more neurotic fraction of my age group. Wales had undergone some pretty momentous ethical changes in the years since the war. The outlook of my parents' generation was forged during the long emergency of the thirties and forties, at a time when most of the country still held fast to the values of nonconformity. To glance at a photograph of industrial Wales from (say) 1945 is to see a spirited, resourceful and talented people in the grip of a moral incubus that stymied all their best instincts – punitive, cripplingly puritanical, intent on inducing shame. By the time I was born the hour of consumerism had struck. A culture that had once prescribed self-denial at all costs now enjoined us to emote, imbibe and copulate in the service of planned obsolescence. Yet things had not changed entirely. The old ways still exerted a restraining grip on the new. The moral tensions that disfigured family life were as severe as any since the 1920s. My own parents were intelligent, humorous and easygoing but there were aspects of the new order that they could scarcely be expected to understand. The promiscuous, the raucous and the ostentatious were not to their taste and they didn't care who knew it. Virtually everyone else of their age felt the same. Those of us who came after had to decide where we stood.

For me at least (and I suspect for many other children born to upwardly mobile parents) the choice between different forms of morality had an inescapably spatial dimension. The polarity between old and new seemed especially stark because I came to associate it with different areas of Wales. Let me try and give you some sense of what I mean. During my childhood we often visited my paternal grandmother in her imposing stone house in a mining village in the South Wales valleys. (Actually it would be more accurate to say former mining village, since the last pit had shut in the 1960s in spite of boasting what the locals liked to call the 'best anthracite in the world'.) The drive from Swansea only took three quarters of an hour but always involved the most violent feelings of displacement. Even now, *pace* Wordsworth, it is difficult to recollect them in tranquillity. Heading out from Swansea in the back of my parents' car, grimly aware that I had four or five hours of familial duty ahead of me, I was always struck by the city's *up-to-dateness.* For all that people joked about its shabby provincialism or invoked Dylan Thomas's line about the 'ugly, lovely town', it visibly belonged to what the French sometimes call *la société de consommation.* The texture of its commercial sector was everywhere defined by plate glass, concrete, chrome and plastic. Advertising hoardings touted personal transformation at very reasonable prices. Not even the subliminal hiss from the sea could disguise the fact that culture had triumphed over nature.

The quiet roads that carried us out to the valleys spoke of a very different Wales. Even thirty years later I slip into the idiom of some gloomy Baptist preacher whenever I call them to mind. The mere thought of those fields, mountains and factories has me raving on about God and man conspiring to depress the spirit. I suppose the basic problem was that two centuries of heavy industry had added a new layer of bleakness to an already sullen landscape. The mechanical and the organic had met in mortal combat and neither side had walked away unscathed. These days the outward signs of coalmining have all but disappeared. In those days the slag heaps, chimneys and pithead wheels leeched the life out of everything. The fields flanking the road always seemed wan and uncultivated, dotted here and there by a pony or a tethered goat. In my memory the only people one ever sees are stooping men in raincoats and middle-aged washerwomen smoking Woodbines. Later I would come to recognise the vitality, intelligence and courage that illuminated the valleys like a Chinese lantern, but all I could see at the time was the greyness, the depression, the lack of hope. Even so there was something about it I liked. In the throes of adolescent self-consciousness I couldn't escape the suspicion that life in the valleys was somehow worthier – somehow more *authentic* – than life in the affluent suburbs. The city glistered like gold but the industrial villages offered a high road to the soul. Inwardness was all.

The point I'm making is that the geographical and the moral were powerfully intertwined in my boyish imagination. Swansea and the valleys served as binary symbols of two very different world views. I associated the village with probity, decency and self-denial and the city with flightiness, decadence and self-indulgence. The problem I had was that both sets of qualities seemed equally compelling and utterly incompatible. Should I be virtuous or licentious? Did the brooding seriousness of the chapel outweigh the emotional high of the record shop? Was it better to honour the body or abuse it? It is astonishing how much importance an unworldly boy of thirteen or fourteen can ascribe to questions like these. My contemporaries in the early 1980s divided into three groups according to their attitude towards them. Most of them embraced the prospect of excess with alacrity, dismissing the occasional pang of conscience as a meaningless atavism. A much smaller number violently denounced the decadence of the age and cultivated a curious mixture of religious ardour, intellectual intensity and virginal reproachfulness. The rest of us (for this was the group to which I belonged) oscillated between the cheerfully louche and the prissily ethical and never quite decided which side we should take. Part of me believed that a few acts of moral turpitude would have devastating consequences for the state of my mortal soul. Another part suspected that the moral dangers of sex, drugs and rock and roll had been wildly overstated. Awkwardly suspended between two moral poles – too lacking in gumption or personality to take a firm view and stick with it – I spent far too long contemplating my ethical navel when I should have been living.

I don't want to overstate the case. I suffered no Gandhian agonies in my efforts to wrestle with these problems. But the pain of living under two moral dispensations at the same time was often considerable. One of the ways I dealt with it was to go out on extremes. Unaware that I was slowly burdening myself with a reputation for witless eccentricity, I took the prevailing ideas of decency and indecency and twisted them into absurd parodies of themselves. On the one hand I set myself up as quite the little gentleman. Influenced by dim memories of the public-school novels I'd devoured as a boy, I cultivated a sort of mock-seigneurial politeness which came across as risibly unnatural. No one else in Wales ever used the terms 'nice to meet you', 'I didn't mean to be rude' and 'I'm exceptionally sorry' as often as I did. Nor was this all. There were times when I pursued the ideal of decency with an almost monastic rigour. For weeks at a time I'd give up some harmless pleasure like rock music, television or staring at girls' breasts, convinced that my soul needed cleansing before it was too late. The only problem was that my addiction to these things became all the more emphatic once my will finally broke.

The obverse side of all this decency was a maniacal liking for the puerile, the obscene and the confessional. At no stage did I ever experiment with booze, drugs or underage sex. My puritanism would not have allowed it and at any rate my scornful contemporaries made it clear that Dionysian excess was not for the likes of me. Instead I sublimated the more intemperate side of my character into a sort of manic childishness. Whenever I went out with my friends my main purpose was always to shatter boyish taboos. Shuffling along besides serious young-men-in-the-making who valued their dignity above all else, I ceaselessly tried to tempt them into revealing their most embarrassing secrets. Whom were they secretly in love with? Did they own any porno mags and how did they hide them from their parents? How often did they stoop to self-abuse? The answer to these questions were of no interest to me. What I relished were the red-faced protests which confirmed that my imputations of indecency had hit home. As pure in body as it was possible for an adolescent boy to be, I nevertheless regarded myself as a subversive messenger from the lower depths. Incapable of realising my own desires, I could only cope with the frustration by reminding the more mannerly people around me that they too were in the grip of the gutter. It goes without saying that my language was always foul.

By the time I reached fourteen I realised that something had to give. The continuous transitions between pristine decency and supercharged profanity were beginning to exhaust me. Somewhere in my mind I knew that a lifetime of self-denial could only lead to the death of the spirit – the emotional anaemia of so many of my teachers proved *that* all too clearly – but at the same time I'd grown rather ashamed of my juvenile delight in swear words, ribaldry and innuendo. In retrospect I can see that my strategy for coping with my split identity involved a textbook case of projection. Intent on freeing myself from the ascetic on the one hand and the debauched on the other (not that I knew too much about the latter), I took to thinking of them as properties of the external world which impinged on my life but did not fundamentally belong to it. Never exactly at ease outside the family home, I now regarded the 'real world' as an infinitely threatening space where people either withered from indulging themselves too little or sold their souls by indulging themselves too much. The next step was to think of my private world as a sort of enchanted haven from the temptations and dangers that existed outside. Holding the idea of pleasure at arm's length but not rejecting it completely, I came to feel that mankind's highest purpose (I actually spoke in these terms) was to batten down the hatches against the storm. The goal was to carve out a radiant 'here' that would sustain the soul against the onslaught of 'there'. Monstrously self-dramatising though I undoubtedly was, I became a sincere convert to the doctrine of redemptive retreat – retreat into warm womblike rooms, the whisky-like embrace of literature (I was going through my poetic period) and the whispered endearments of pale gentle girls. Asked to define love in a classroom discussion of Shakespeare's sonnets, I said that 'love is what the spirit does in response to adversity'. I had never heard the term but my view of the world was manichaean through and through. Everything boiled down to the battle between good and evil.

Does all this embarrass me now? Certainly. But embarrassment is beside the point. The thing about my callow adolescent musings was that they prepared the ground for everything that came next. The fourteen-year-old boy who stares out from that photo in his aunt's garden is a strange case indeed. Born into a loving home and given more opportunities than he deserved, he has failed quite spectacularly to make a go of things. His most salient characteristics are a sentimental attachment to the working class and a tendency to think of the world in terms of moral extremes. On the face of it he has no prospects and no hope. He is perfect fodder for the dream weavers of the Hard Left.

CHAPTER 2
Anarchy, for a While

There was a time in the 1990s when I not only bought the *New Statesman* every week but actually took the trouble to read it. My favourite part was a weekly feature in which prominent people on the left responded to a questionnaire. In one issue a young radical journalist, now largely known for serving up centrist clichés in the *Mail on Sunday*, answered the question 'Which event in your lifetime has had the biggest impact on your political beliefs?' by simply saying 'Punk'. I knew exactly what she meant.

My friend Julian and I caught the bus from Swansea at about six in the evening. The sky had already darkened but the air was warm with the promise of spring. The journey to the Sandfields Estate in Port Talbot was due to take an hour, though the bus driver lingered for ages at the station while he smoked a cigarette. Julian and I were both appropriately dressed for the master class in subversion that awaited us. He wore a battered leather jacket, a pair of black canvas trousers and suede boots. I had also opted for black canvas trousers but topped them off with a mohair jumper and a Portuguese army jacket. We both sported CND badges in our lapels. We were just short of fifteen and regarded ourselves as serious enemies of the state.

The route to Port Talbot took us through some of South Wales's least affluent areas. It was too dark to see much outside, but when I cupped my eyes to the window I often caught a glimpse of a council house or a factory or a row of cheap shops.

At one point a boy of about eighteen got on and immediately deciphered our sartorial codes. Carrying a rolled-up sleeping bag on his back and wearing only a t-shirt and a pair of ripped jeans (I still don't understand why he hadn't died of hypothermia), he gave us a slightly insolent look and asked 'Are you going to see Crass?' We told him that we were and he came to sit with us. Within seconds he had cadged one of Julian's rolled cigarettes, lovingly conjured from Samson tobacco and green Rizlas.

Crass were the leading band in what the cognoscenti liked to call the 'anarcho-punk' movement. They had been around since 1978 and were a genuine underground phenomenon. Appealing largely to audacious teenage rebels like Julian but occasionally reaching out to lost souls like me, they had condensed the gospel of anarchist-pacifism into a series of coruscating songs and vividly poetic slogans: 'Fight War Not Wars', 'There Is No Authority But Yourself', 'ANOK4U2'. To call oneself a Crass fan was to declare one's opposition to all forms of power. It was to take the side of the common people in their struggle for freedom and social justice. Or something like that. Tonight we would see the band for the first time.

The boy with the sleeping bag wasted no time in establishing his streetsmart credentials. He told us that he'd hitched to the gig from Bristol after being let out early from borstal. 'What were you in for?', I asked. 'Screwing a shop', he replied. (I quickly surmised that Bristolian anarchists regarded 'screw' and 'burgle' as synonyms.) Deducing from our wary looks that Julian and I were less than impressed with this story, he repeated himself almost word-for-word when another Crass fan joined us at the next stop. This time he held his audience in the cradle of his pockmarked arms. The new boy was a slovenly glue sniffer who wore his hooliganism like a pair of bondage trousers. None too articulate but full of edgy conceit, he was desperate to have his hatred of authority reinforced. When the Bristolian told him about his trial, insisting that a custodial sentence was only handed out because the magistrate's wife had overcooked his breakfast, he smirked for a few seconds and said 'You can't call it justice, can you?' The question hung in the air. Part of me wanted to say 'Actually, you can.'

The Sandfields Estate has recently been described in Wikipedia as 'one of the most troubled estates' in Wales. In those days its reputation was even worse. As the four of us got off the bus and walked towards the community centre in which the gig was taking place, I let my imagination get the better of me. I convinced myself that everything Crass opposed had somehow become concentrated in the flats, houses and pubs that clustered around us in the dark. Political malignancy and moral brutishness were everywhere. My paranoid imaginings transformed the estate into a crumbling housing project in inter-war Berlin, somewhere towards the end of the Weimar Republic. Neanderthal fascists patrolled the courtyards in groups of three or four, meting out summary justice to anyone who looked subversive. Mob orators stood on soapboxes and gave incendiary speeches outside cheap restaurants, encouraging their listeners to bring the 'race problem' to a blood-spattered conclusion. Despairing policeman hovered in the shadows, realised that order could never be restored and set off for more law-abiding climes.

Part of me was enjoying it, of course. In the back of my mind I knew perfectly well that those dilapidated streets were too spaced out on lager, cholesterol and valium to incubate the British Reich. Yet the sense of impending crisis proved difficult to shake. It also inspired military metaphors of the most melodramatic kind. I began to think of the gig as a surprise manoeuvre by libertarian guerrillas, a heroic attempt to establish an outpost of enlightenment in the midst of the capitalist beast. The atmosphere outside the community centre did nothing to dissolve my illusions. In truth the punks, skinheads and dropouts who were queuing to get in knew little enough about anarchy, but most of them (or most of us) seemed intent on putting their libertarian ethics into practice. There were no jostlings and no yobbish efforts to jump the queue. Pale and unlettered youths struck up hesitant conversations with each other, made ritual remarks about the shittiness of the government (unemployment was running at 15 per cent in South Wales at the time) and willingly shared cider, tobacco and fanzines. The Bristolian and the glue sniffer shed their macho pretensions. Not even the exterior walls of the centre had escaped the anarchist carnival. Crass had been around in the afternoon and sprayed them with stencilled slogans, one of which (a compressed meditation on the relationship between consumerism and political apathy) unforgettably read 'In All Our Decadence People Die'. I loved the idea that these cryptic messages would linger on the walls for decades, lighting flares of subversion in the distracted minds of passers-by. No doubt they have long since been whitewashed away.

Nothing short of Alzheimer's could wash away the memory of the gig. It was three hours of pure otherness. A few years previously the Sex Pistols had broken rock music's four-minute mile, extruding songs of astonishing speed and ferocity from their rancorous imaginations. Crass had appropriated the formula and added a new level of urgency. It wasn't simply that the songs were faster than anything one had ever heard, played by speeding pistons rather than human limbs. The crucial thing was the ratio of verbiage to melody. As the lead vocalist ruptured his tonsils at the microphone, he seemed to be defying the rest of the band to finish the song before he could spit out his snarling denunciations. Immensely long lines were savagely compressed into a handful of speeding bars. A couplet like 'Black man's got his problems and his way to deal with it/So don't fool yourself you're helping with your white liberal shit' took exactly three seconds to dispatch.[2] Intent on screaming 'No! No! No!' at everything that existed, Crass played like fugitives from 1984 who knew that the Thought Police might break down the door at any minute. It was, as the rock critics like to say, a high-adrenaline experience.

But there was more to it than that. The real importance

2 The couplet here is taken from the song 'White Punks on Dope' on the album *Stations of the Crass* (Crass Records, 1979).

of Crass was that they gestured towards the thrilling open-endedness of the weeks, months and years to come. At any one moment they directed our attention not merely to the present but to two different visions of the future. Most of the lyrics were contemporary in their scope, surveying and denouncing everything from Thatcher, Reagan and Brezhnev to soap operas, tabloid journalists and lorry drivers. But even the simplest song posed a pregnant question: 'Where will all this lead?' As they openly admitted in the letters they wrote to their fans, one of the band's aims was to evoke the texture of a nightmarish totalitarian future.[3] Their method was to warn against fascism by enacting it in front of our eyes. On stage they dressed only in black and stared menacingly into the middle distance. The affectless faces and heavy boots suggested robotic stormtroopers from Leni Riefenstahl's *Triumph of the Will.* The howling guitars, strangulated voices and thundering drums made as much noise as the cheering crowds and guttural oratory at Nuremberg. Be warned – civilisation may be more fragile than you think. That was the simple message.

Or not so simple, as things turned out. Intimations of disaster were always balanced by telegrams from utopia. Julian once challenged me to identify the most 'emblematic' moment on Crass's records. I chose the few seconds at the end of *Christ – The Album* when we hear a snippet from one of E.P. Thompson's magisterial orations in Trafalgar Square: 'I want you to – I want you to SENSE YOUR OWN STRENGTH!' Everything Crass did encouraged us to build bridges to a better future. Change must begin *this second*, or so they told us. The role of the individual is to seek more autonomy in the here and now, in the hope that he will inspire others to do the same. By defying authority and scorning the warmongers and insisting on the right to shape his

3 Crass's bassist Pete Wright once wrote in a letter to a fan that 'A large part of what the band can do is point out, or even give a small indication of the way things are going. Our stage appearance ... is a charade of what people might have to deal with in 5-10-15 years' time.' Quoted in George McKay, *Senseless Acts of Beauty: Cultures of Resistance since the Sixties* (London: Verso, 1996), p. 84.

own existence, he adds to a swelling tide of liberty whose waves will eventually crash on the shores of a free society: 'Be exactly what you want to be – do what you want to do/I am he and she is she but you're the only you.'[4] I'm embarrassed to say that I've been marked by this doctrine for life.

I suspect that many people only saw the darker side of Crass, but evidence of their utopianism was anywhere and everywhere. A handful of their songs were as delicate and numinous as Chinese poetry, using imagery from the natural world to hint at humanity's instinctive yearning for freedom. Even the more cacophonous material was dense enough to subvert its own negativity. Time and again a guitar riff or a passage of electronic noise broke free from the *mêlée* and pottered around on the margins of a song, rejoicing in its liberty like an unsupervised child. At gigs the band would mingle with the audience and chat about anything that came to mind. No one knew much about them. They had long since symbolised their faith in the power of self-determination by endowing themselves with new names. There was a Steve Ignorant and a Phil Free and an Eve Libertine and a Gee Vaucher and even an N.A. Palmer. Pete Wright sometimes called himself Pete Wrong and Joy de Vivre occasionally opted for Virginia Creeper. It says a lot for the band's commitment to gender politics that Penny Rimbaud, its drummer and ideologue, was actually a man.

The last song that night was the anthemic 'Do They Owe us a Living?', which famously answered itself with a resounding 'Of course they fucking do!' The band melted away and a bright light illuminated the anarchist banners at the back of the stage. Then a brief piece of film was projected onto a backdrop. Images of goose-stepping soldiers and ruined cities gave way to sunlit fields, flowers and newly born children. For the last time we were offered a choice between despair and hope. In my adolescent way I devoted my life to hope and took my leave of the hall, exchanging superlatives with Julian. The night had one last surprise in store for us. In the car park a punk was selling

4 Crass, 'Big A, Little A', B-side of the single *Nagasaki Nightmare* (Crass Records, 1980).

an anarchist fanzine with a photo of Crass on the cover. The last copy was sold to a rough-looking boy of about thirteen, who proceeded to show it off to his friends. Seconds later he was screaming with fury as the Bristolian with the sleeping bag snatched it away from him.

'Give it back – I just paid for that!'

'Shut the fuck up', replied the Bristolian. 'What would you know about anarchism anyway? Be a good boy and run off back to mummy – this 'zine belongs to me.'

———

Why am I telling you all this? In part because nostalgia is one of my abiding sins, and nothing makes me more nostalgic than the thought of that distant night on the Sandfields Estate. But there's another reason as well. If people of a certain age and a certain cast of mind like nothing better than recounting their punk stories, it's precisely because punk was one of modern culture's great catalysts. It served as an introduction to some pretty momentous things. Its mission was to grab guileless adolescents by the scruff of the neck and afford them a tantalising glimpse of art, politics and the mysteries of the self. Those of us who responded to these glimpses often found that our life's work had been mapped out without our knowing it. Punk produced writers, artists, musicians and world-class eccentrics by the bucketload. It also produced radicals – hundreds of them. Scarcely any of the people who attended the Crass gig that night would call themselves anarchists today, but I'd wager that quite a few graduated to the Marxist sects and remain with them even now. Punk gave us our first intimation of what it meant to be on the left. It took our emotional dispositions and cultural prejudices and filled them with political content. Its attitudes shaped our encounter with more serious forms of politics. In that sense we owe it everything.

Let me put it this way. For a few weeks in 1982 I defined myself as an anarchist and a pacifist. I had never read a single anarchist text, though I'd tried my best with the first fifteen pages of Giovanni Baldelli's *Social Anarchism*. What I *had* done was listen to Crass records every day for weeks. My ideological conversion was solely down to them. Even at the time the fine print of the anarchist vision worried me greatly. Try as I might I just couldn't accept that a world without the state could ever be stable – I mean, what would I do if someone stole my records? But rationality wasn't what the game was about. Punk worked directly on the adrenal glands, unleashing tidal waves of excitement because its vision of politics corresponded (or seemed to correspond) with attitudes I already held. It confirmed my identity in the very act of transforming it.

Take the issue of class. As it happens, Crass weren't really exponents of the class struggle. In one song they went so far as to say that they'd 'Heard too much about the people in the ghetto/Heard too much about the working-class motto.'[5] Yet their apoplectic hatred of elites and mystical faith in the 'people' was populist to the core. The realisation that there were other people who venerated the subaltern classes (a phrase I wouldn't have used at the time) was revelatory in itself. It also made me recognise that my casual sympathy for tramps, dropouts and workers brought responsibilities in its wake. After listening to Crass's violent attacks on what they liked to call the 'system', it no longer seemed enough to spare 50p and a comradely word for a member of the homeless. In some sense I had to take my stand against all the bastards who created this misery in the first place. To be an anarchist was to face the possibility that one day, after all the 'grey puke' of late capitalism had been hosed down, those tramps and drunks and workers who populated my imagination might actually *run society*. It was heady and terrifying stuff.

Then there was the question of morality. As I have tried to show, I had arrived by the age of fourteen or fifteen at a highly manichaean view of the world. Anxious to reconcile the asceticism of my parents' generation with consumerist injunctions to seek pleasure at all costs, I concluded that the duty of human beings was to carve out small redemptive spaces in the face of an overwhelmingly oppressive world. (The word

5 Crass, *Heard Too Much About* on *Stations of the Crass.*

'duty' came naturally to my dogmatic teenage lips.) One of the things that obsessed me about punk was that it took these manichaean intuitions and politicised them. Consciously or otherwise it divided the world into two opposed terrains. The terrain of the 'system' was intolerably sinister and extended nearly everywhere, oozing death, acquisitiveness and repression from every pore. Merely to set foot in a workplace or a school or a shop was to risk having one's spirit cauterised forever. Opposed to the system were the few spaces we had shaped for ourselves – bedrooms, communes, rehearsal halls and streets in which the spirit of anarchy prevailed. This side of the revolution the only responsible thing to do was to shun the mainstream like a plague.

Nearly everyone who took anarcho-punk seriously seemed to think in these terms, even those of us who didn't look like punks and would never have had the temerity to try. Here again it was Crass who shaped our perceptions. Their genius was to create arresting metaphors (or should that be metonymies?) for the dark spaces of the system and the radiant enclaves of anarchist resistance. Their signature tactic was to associate capitalism with the culture of the modern city. They continually underscored the system's inhumanity by throwing out images of rundown houses, trashy shops, sinister advertisements and brutal acts of violence in backstreets or alleys. In front of me as I write is Gee Vaucher's extraordinary photomontage for the cover of *The Feeding of the 5000*, Crass's first and most popular release.[6] It is the *ne plus ultra* of punk's urban paranoia. In the background we see a row of derelict terraced houses. There is no possibility that the electricity is still connected, though we notice that two young boys are watching television in the ruins. Out in front is a patch of waste ground where civilised life seems to be breaking down. Men in cheap suits warm themselves in front of a fire. A female mannikin stands perfectly upright but is singed from head to toe. An abandoned child sits shirtless

6 The cover of *The Feeding of the 5000* is reproduced in Gee Vaucher, *Crass Art and other Pre-Postmodernist Monsters* (Edinburgh: AK Press and Exitstencil Press, 1999), p. 28.

in the rubble, flanked by soldiers from unidentifiable regiments who hover with their weapons at the ready. The image is at once curiously familiar and bafflingly ambiguous. Is it a scene from Northern Ireland or an evocation of a nuclear holocaust? Is it a protest against the city or a plea for its reconstruction? In the end it is all of these things and nothing. Vaucher's message is that dereliction is *everywhere*. The city reflects the system and the system reflects the city.

But what of our zones of resistance, those blessed plots where the black flag of anarchy had already begun to flutter? There were areas in every city which the anarcho-punks tried to colonise, but Crass left us in no doubt that their own home was the ideal we should aspire to. All the members of the band lived at Dial House, a sixteenth-century cottage on the edge of Epping Forest. Penny Rimbaud had rented it in 1967, laboured long and hard to rescue it from disrepair and then opened it as a commune. Standing in substantial gardens and hidden at the end of a long lane, it figured (and perhaps figures) in the anarchist imagination as a message of hope from the future. Dial House was anarchy in action. Like the gardens at Ermenonville which Rousseau immortalised in the eighteenth century, it was a place where the deepest needs of the mind were uncannily reflected in the landscape. There was no rigid distinction between the inner and the outer. The gardens were innocent of territorial divisions and extended right through to the living spaces. Driftwood, rocks and plants proliferated in the bedrooms and the kitchen. Expansive lawns alternated with shaded grottoes, mysterious sheds and ramshackle flowerbeds. Visitors have almost killed themseves trying to describe the curiously ethereal atmosphere. The best I can do is to say that everything seemed lightly brushed with celestial varnish. Imagine that the visions of some enraptured nature mystic – a Wordsworth or a Traherne or a Coleridge – had seeped into the soil and bathed everything in their pure white light. That's what Dial House was like.

Perhaps. Although scores of people have passed through the place over the last forty years, I have never been one of them. My impressions of Dial House are based on a handful of photographs, a chapter in C.J. Stone's *Fierce Dancing* and the writings of Penny Rimbaud. And the point about Rimbaud is that he's a mythographer of rare gifts. His recollections of Dial House are so well crafted that they continually make the improbable ring true. One in particular sticks in everyone's mind. Back in the 1970s, or so the story goes, Rimbaud was a close friend of a *soi-disant* shaman, activist and hippie called Phil Russell.[7] The two first met when Russell turned up in the garden on a hot summer morning. Waving cheerfully at Rimbaud, who was staring out of the kitchen window, he skipped behind a shed and reappeared a second later with a snowstorm suspended between his hands. For a few moments a small expanse of Essex sky was as white and turbulent as the roof of Everest. Then Russell went back behind the shed and the weather returned to normal.[8]

When I first heard this story I was seized by ambivalence. A shiver ran down my spine but I also felt slightly queasy. What on earth was Rimbaud doing? Why was he inflicting this mystical nonsense on his youthful admirers? Wasn't he aware that religion was the mortal foe of the liberated mind? But then my sense of wonder got the better of me. The thought of Russell directing the weather like a long-haired Prometheus seemed too poignant for words. I began to conceive of his snowstorm as the spirit of a wise magus, separated forever from the brain that had once encased it. 'If this story isn't true', I said to myself, 'it bloody well ought to be.'

An early lesson in ideology?

---

7 Phil Russell (1947-1975), also known as Wally Hope, played a central role in organising the Windsor Free Festivals and the Stonehenge Free Festivals in the early 1970s. Penny Rimbaud has always maintained that he was murdered by the state.

8 See Penny Rimbaud, *Shibboleth: My Revolting Life* (Edinburgh: AK Press, 1998), p. 64. Cf. Penny Rimbaud, Pete Wright and Mick Duffield, *A Series of Shock Slogans and Mindless Token Tantrums* (London: Exitstencil Press, 1982), pp. 21-22; C.J. Stone, *Fierce Dancing: Adventures in the Underground* (London: Faber and Faber, 1996), pp. 80-81.

Contradictions began to hove into view. The thrill of radical commitment was blunted, though only for a few seconds at the dead of night, by a handful of nagging questions. The purpose of the anarchist was to change society, or so I'd been told. The revolution would not be complete until the last monetarist had been hanged from a lamppost by the entrails of the last disc jockey. So why the persistent duality between the system's spaces and ours? Wasn't our reverence for Dial House and all the other 'free places' simply an exercise in parochialism, an excuse to tend our own (organic) gardens and not take our message to the people? These issues remained with me.

Other sorts of inconsistency also began to grate. In my naiveté I supposed that anarchists abhorred power and that pacifists eschewed violence. But the thought of that Bristolian with the fanzine was difficult to shift. His shameless combination of imperiousness and physical force was quite something. Could it be possible that professing radicalism was easier than achieving virtue? Might it be the case that professing radicalism sometimes *undermined* virtue? Could I say with my hand on my heart that my own impulses were as pristine as I liked to pretend? These issues too would continue to weigh heavily.

There was one person in the spring of 1982 who did more than anyone else to crystallise my anxieties. He was known as 'Mastiff' and he was Swansea's most recognisable punk. No one doubted his commitment to the cause. A versatile hairdresser had cropped his hair all over but left a two-inch fringe dangling over his forehead. The bristles on his scalp were yellow on one side and black on the other. His leather jacket was invariably worn over a Sex Pistols t-shirt and suffered from an excess of semiosis. Virtually the whole expanse of it was given over to badges, patches, stencilled slogans and garish street art. Plastered across the back was an image of flesh melting from an angular face while a mushroom cloud loomed overhead. The caption, echoing one of CND's most powerful slogans of the time, simply read 'Protest and Survive'. When the younger punks swarmed around him in Virgin Records on a Saturday afternoon, they agreed that nothing would stop Mastiff getting his message across. He was an anarchist to the scuffed tips of his Doctor Marten boots.

And yet. Early in the spring his behaviour got odder and he began to attract dark rumours. He and his girlfriend would often appear on the streets with crimson weals on their faces, necks and hands. She in particular looked as ashen as a snowdrop and rarely spoke. At the time the two of them were living in a bedsit on one of the steep hills overlooking the city. People started saying that if you stood outside late at night (not that anyone admitted to doing so), you could hear strange noises coming through the window: whips cracking, flesh smarting, voices crying in pained ecstasy. As if to confirm the gossip, Mastiff began appearing in public with a riding crop thrown over his shoulder. The acronym BDSM was mysteriously added to his jacket. In those days there was no internet to tell us what it meant.

Things moved quickly after that. A breakdown worthy of Dostoevsky was compressed into little more than two months. Mastiff's girlfriend moved out of the bedsit and went back to live with her parents. Her distraught boyfriend was seen in the centre of Swansea walking a goat on the end of a lead. Then his appearance changed dramatically. His mania for making statements began to colonise his skin. Tattoos appeared on his neck and spread rapidly across his cheeks and forehead. One afternoon I stole a glance at him as he paraded drunkenly down Union Street. He looked for all the world like a sort of stylised AIDS victim, a man near death whose face was consumed by images rather than tumours. In his hand he carried a copy of *The Confessions of Aleister Crowley*. This was a clue to the ludicrous dénouement, though I didn't realise it at the time.

It turned out that Mastiff had acquired exorbitant metaphysical ambitions. He'd been experimenting with LSD, seen God on a particularly fraught trip and begun to question the distinction between mind and matter. He told his friends that he could bend the entire world to his will simply through the power of thought. Reaganism, apartheid, fascism in El Salvador – there was nothing he couldn't overcome if the psychic energies were flowing in the right direction. His brief reign as an anarcho-occultist came to a humiliating end towards the middle of July. When the police went to his old school in the middle of the night (they were responding to a call from a member of the public), they found him in the chemistry labs performing an elaborate magical ritual. He was wearing his girlfriend's bra, his mother's knickers and a pair of fishnet stockings whose ownership has never been determined. The story was all over Swansea within twenty-four hours.

My response to all this was one of distaste rather than comprehension. I couldn't really understand why Mastiff behaved in the way he did, but the stench of spiritual decay lingered in my nostrils for days. With some part of my mind I realised that Mastiff's breakdown couldn't simply be blamed on a badly wired brain or a calamitous upbringing. In one way or another it was directly linked to his radical posturings. The leering sociopath who whipped his girlfriend until she bled, terrified pedestrians with his facial tattoos and called down curses on the whole of mankind was the same man (or boy) who had set himself up as Swansea's biggest apostle of freedom. But what was the nature of the link?

Several years later, in the middle of what turned out to be an abortive research project on radical subcultures, I began to descry an answer. The unlikely source of illumination was Greil Marcus's *Lipstick Traces*, a massive work of 'secret history' which relates punk to earlier radical movements such as Situationism, Lettrisme, Dadaism and even the Brethren of the Free Spirit. Marcus's argument is that all these movements were bound together by their 'negationist' sensibility.[9] Obsessed with establishing a truly free society, they sought to abolish the existing order by creating the impression that *everything* was open to change. The medium of their revolt was a sort of incandescent

9 See Greil Marcus, *Lipstick Traces: A Secret History of the Twentieth Century* (London: Secker and Warburg, 1989).

negativity. By hurling impassioned abuse at everything in their line of vision, they affirmed that 'natural facts' were no less corrigible than 'historical constructs'. They believed that the body, the weather and the immemorial truths of human nature could be overthrown as easily as the government – an outlook memorably summed up by Johnny Rotten in the Sex Pistols' song *Bodies* when he urged us to 'Fuck this and fuck that/Fuck it all and fuck a fucking brat.'

Like most punks, Mastiff was a negationist to the core. In all likelihood that was the source of his problems. The great paradox of negationism, as Marcus implies in some of the most overlooked passages of his book, is that eventually it transforms its libertarian exponents into their worst political enemies. Faced with the awful realisation that some things really can't be changed, they begin to experience the most violent feelings of frustration. Their hunger for freedom slowly gives way to an overhelming need to dominate. At first they try to divert this need into harmless channels, so as not to compromise their political ideals. The yearning to be obeyed, to say 'Do as I wish or else!', is expressed in some purely personal context, as when Mastiff transformed his bedsit into a sexual torture chamber. Then comes the phase of bodily agony. Nothing torments the negationist more horribly than the intractable solidities of his own body. When Mastiff covered his face with tattoos, or so I've come to think, he was gripped by the delusion that his genes could be altered simply by crucifying the skin. The turn to religion was all but inevitable. Enslaved by an exigent desire to transcend the physical world, Mastiff capped his ruination by investing in the myth of his own psychic greatness. The role of the women's underwear remains unclear.

Mastiff's disappearance from the scene taught me a great deal. It confirmed my suspicion that radicalism was easier to proclaim than to achieve. It reminded me that men should never experiment with lace panties. And it forced me to realise that anarchism wasn't really my thing. I began to look around for something better suited to my personality – something less extreme and more serious but equally *engagé*. It came along soon enough.

A word about Julian. At first sight he and I made a pretty unlikely pair. Everyone in the lousy comprehensive school in which we met regarded us as polar opposites. He was one of the fourth form's rebels – brooding, experienced with cigarettes and condoms, deeply attractive to girls. I was a bland conformist with a fatuously genial disposition and no compensating vices of any kind. But none of that seemed to matter. For a couple of years we sustained the sort of intense, quixotic and cheerfully pretentious teenage friendship that transforms stray subversive impulses into fully fledged radical commitments. No one did more to turn me into a socialist than Julian did.

The thing that first brought us together was our fascination with punk. One lunchtime I was eating a sandwich in the school canteen when I overheard Julian, who was sitting opposite me with a fearsomely sullen skinhead friend, talking about the Crass album *Penis Envy*. On a whim I caught his gaze and told him that I'd been listening to the album the previous evening (which was true) and that my favourite track was 'Where Next Columbus?' The memory of his less-than-effusive response still makes me laugh. Temporarily thrown off balance by the thought that anyone as wet as me could even have heard of Crass, he looked me up and down with burning contempt but for some reason felt obliged to spare me a few words. He agreed that 'Where Next Columbus?' was terrific but insisted that 'Bata Motel' was even better. After a few more desultory exchanges he drained his cup of tea with an exaggerated slurp and stalked off into the yard. I had no reason to suppose that we would ever speak to each other again.

But we did. From time to time we bumped into each other in the corridors and surprised ourselves by taking up our conversation where it had left off. Right from the start there was a strange sense of mutual recognition that overrode Julian's scorn and short-circuited my nervousness. Soon enough we were deep in the throes of co-conspiracy. Every Saturday we met in a dingy café in Swansea and spent the rest of the day strutting about like aspirant *flâneurs*. I realise now that the cement in our relationship was our shared anxiety about social status. Like me – though on a much more emphatic, sod-you-all scale – Julian was a disaffected member of the second-generation middle class. His parents had risen from humble backgrounds in the valleys to make it big in education, and though he was highly intelligent (precociously so, in fact) he harboured serious doubts about his capacity to follow their example. From the age of about ten he had gone spectacularly off the rails, playing truant from school whenever he could and embracing all the activities – smoking, drinking, parading menacingly in the streets – that marked a child out in those days as an agent of the devil. His suspicion of bourgeois respectability and sentimental regard for the workers were as pronounced as my own. Ours was the solidarity of two well-to-do kids determined to squander every opportunity we had been given.

The influence we exerted on each other was mutual but Julian was always a bigger deal in my life than I was in his. What I got from him was the opportunity to mix with a truly vital, truly creative person for the first time. What he got from me was a streak of wide-eyed enthusiasm that enabled him to put his more unorthodox plans into practice. Before we met he was always too self-conscious to immerse himself in the anarchist scene, in spite of the fact that his love of punk and his natural hatred of authority made him yearn to do so. Within two months of that awkward encounter in the canteen we had both reinvented ourselves as novitiate Bakunins, egging each other on in our relentlessly juvenile attempts to bring the state to its knees. One day he told me out of the blue that he'd been 'much more militant' since our friendship had begun. It was one of the proudest moments of my emotionally incontinent life.

Because we came to politics relatively young – at least by the standards of our prosaic contemporaries – our early efforts at subversion lacked a certain gravitas. Influenced by dimly understood articles in anarchist cultural journals, we believed that the most effective political acts were those which combined propaganda with entertainment. Spectacle mattered more than the fine print of our political vision. One of our favourite stunts was to scream libertarian slogans at passing policemen and then disappear down an alleyway before we got caught. Another was to walk into an army recruitment office and silently hand a copy of *Peace News* to the person in charge. Inevitably, however, we spent the bulk of our time trying to make music. The anarcho-punk scene was rooted in the premise that anyone could form a band. By dismantling the distinction between audience and performer – by exploding the myth that some people possess musical talent while others do not – we believed that we could rid the world of artistic hierarchies as a step towards ridding it of political power. The five-piece band I founded with Julian was called Caveat Emptor, a name which testified to Julian's immense suspicion of commercial culture as well as his surprisingly extensive knowledge of Latin. The project was by no means a success. Perhaps the kindest thing I can say is that we laboured manfully to expose the flaws in the punk orthodoxy. It turned out that not everyone could make music after all.

In the chilly spring of 1982, shortly before the Falklands crisis breathed new life into Mrs Thatcher's administration and broke the hearts of teenage anarchists across Britain, Caveat Emptor played its one and only gig. At the time there was a bikers' pub on Wind Street where bands played every evening except Sunday. Its real name was the Coach and Horses but for some reason everyone called it the Coach House. Late one Wednesday night I received an agitated phonecall from Ernie, Caveat Emptor's worryingly out-of-control lead singer, who confessed that he'd persuaded the landlord to let us do a few songs before the regular band took to the stage on Friday. It was no good pointing out that we had less than forty-eight hours to prepare and that we only had three songs in our repertoire, one of which was an atonal instrumental called *In Case of Nuclear Attack*. Ernie insisted that this was our big chance to 'spread our message' and that the other members of the band were really excited about it. The gig must go ahead.

Our first problem was how to get what little equipment we possessed to the venue. In the end we stole two shopping trolleys from Tesco and headed off to Wind Street with our guitars, drums and solitary amplifier piled up in it. On the way we were stopped by two policeman – sinister but genial enforcers of a corrupt system – who demanded proof that the equipment actually belonged to us. As Julian and I sat on the edge of the pavement while Ernie negotiated on our behalf, several buses passed by and every single passenger turned to see what was going on. I sent up a silent prayer that none of my parents' friends had been among them.

We finally arrived at the Coach House much later than we were supposed to, full of theatrical indignation over our encounter with the coercive apparatuses of the state. It turned out that our reputation preceded us. Apparently a rival punk band had spread a rumour to the effect that we always smashed up the venues in which we played. The fact that we had never done a gig before was neither here nor there. The landlord told us that we weren't welcome on his premises and that we should get out before he reported us for underage drinking. Ernie remonstrated with him for ten minutes or so and then went storming off down the street, pausing occasionally to kick a car door or slam the side of his fist against a streetlight. All of us were anxious that he'd gone to get a few lowlife mates to help him sort the landlord out – even at the age of fourteen he had a long record of utterly gratuitous violence – but when he got back he seemed to have perked up considerably. Appalled at the thought that he wouldn't get a chance to put his vocal gifts on display, he'd gone into the Borough Arms at the bottom of Wind Street and asked them whether they needed a band for the evening. 'Hurry up, comrades', he urged. 'We're due onstage in an hour'.

I can remember very little of what happened next, not because I was drunk but because the mismatch between band and venue was the stuff of cultural nightmares. The Borough Arms was the very last place where a bunch of talentless young anarchists should have made their debut. Shamelessly squalid and as dark as Fagin's lair, it catered primarily to hardened alcoholics in their fifties whose enormous sideburns harked back to the glory days of the teddy boys. Most of them had yet to acknowledge that Elvis was dead let alone that punk was a force in the land. Expecting to hear some rousing goodtime music from their youth, they looked on uncomprehendingly as we barked out our dark warnings about power, profit and war. Yet right at the start – before our status as anarchist killjoys had been laid bare – there was a marvellous moment of unity between Caveat Emptor and its audience which still figures in my memory as a sort of farcical symbol of everything punk stood for. Twenty minutes before we were due to start our set, Julian and I decided to perform a soundcheck while the other members of the band got tanked up at the bar. While Julian adjusted the tension on his snare drum I strapped on my guitar, plugged it in and tuned up. Then, anxious to test out the pub's acoustics, I turned the volume up all the way and struck a single emphatic chord. At that point all hell broke loose. The old soaks in front of us let out a cataclysmic roar and started banging their pints against the bar. It could only mean one thing: *They thought the gig had already begun.* In a rare moment of musical co-ordination – knowing full well that we couldn't stop playing now – Julian and I launched into the first song on the setlist while I raced to the microphone and appealed to the other members of the band to join us. The sight of them scrambling onto the stage provoked another merry outburst from the crowd, and for a few seconds the cheers almost drowned out the music. I beamed incredulously at Julian and he beamed incredulously back at me. It was the only time I've ever held a working-class audience in the palms of my hands.

CHAPTER 3
A Squatter in the House of Marx

Julian and I were in the same class for physics, though both of us could go for months at a time without learning anything. My ignorance of Newton's laws of motion is still prodigious. At the beginning of one lesson, opening a conversation that would continue surreptitiously for the next hour, Julian told me that Crass were intending to split up in 1984. 'It's because of the book', he explained. I had no idea what he was talking about but I nodded sagely all the same. Stupidity was one thing. Admitting to it was quite another.

A few days later I asked my father whether he'd heard of a book that had 'something to do with 1984'. He told me that he had and that he owned a copy. He left the table where we'd been eating our Sunday dinner, went to the bookshelves in the passageway and returned with a paperback. 'It's by George Orwell,' he said, 'Haven't you heard of him?' I admitted that I hadn't. Over the next couple of days I read the book in a fit of unlettered awe. If I tell you that everything started there, I don't mean to sound portentous or solipsistic. I realise that the statement is only of interest to me. That doesn't make it any the less true.

Nineteen Eighty-Four wasn't the first book to afford me a glimpse of the past, but it was certainly the first to beckon me into another age and then close the door behind me. Its function in my life was to induct me into History with a capital 'H'. My father's edition had been published by Penguin in 1954, three years after the first majority Labour government had been bundled out of office. Its appearance pointed back to the age of austerity rather than forward to the consumer apocalypse of the 1960s. Even before I scanned its pages it gave off a reverberant echo of the day before yesterday. The paper was coarse and musty and the spine had been tanned by an excess of glue. In conformity with most other Penguin paperbacks in those lost years of literary standardisation, the cover was divided into three horizontal panels like a sort of modernist sandwich. Clarity and simplicity had obviously been the order of the day. The top panel was orange and bore the words 'Penguin Books'. The next one down was white and revealed the title and the author's name. The bottom panel reverted to orange and showed the Penguin colophon flanked by the words 'Complete' and 'Unabridged'. It was an interesting reminder that what seems modern to one age often seems antiquated to another.

Or not so antiquated, as the case may be. My tatty copy of *Nineteen Eighty-Four* was undoubtedly old-fashioned but it wasn't a museum piece. Its title alone emitted a pungent whiff of the here and now. The very fact that it belonged to my father, who had only reached his fifties about a year earlier, suggested that its contemporary relevance had yet to be exhausted. As I held the book in my hands I got the unnerving feeling that past, present and future had somehow been conflated. In one way or another that relic of history was telling me *how to live now*. My sense of moving back and forth between different epochs was powerfully reinforced when I settled down to read. Orwell's prose was arrestingly futuristic and quaintly archaic at the same time. On the first page alone he told us that the 'clocks were striking thirteen' but that the hallway of Victory Mansions 'smelt of boiled cabbage and old rag mats'.[10] And that wasn't all. It soon became clear that the relationship between past and present was part of what the book was about. The Oceanian regime continually told its subjects that life had improved dramatically when Big Brother came to power. In a desperate effort to prove it wrong, Winston Smith immersed

10 George Orwell, *Nineteen Eighty-Four* (London: Penguin, 2000 [1949]), p. 3.

himself in fragile memories of the days before the revolution. Vague but roseate images of his vanished mother invaded his days and dreams. In strict defiance of Party dogma he cherished bric-a-brac and scraps of verbiage from the prelapsarian past – a glass paperweight, a luxurious cream writing book, the first few lines of 'Oranges and Lemons'. Whenever he allowed his mind to focus on these things, it wasn't nostalgia but burning revolutionary zeal that spurred him on. By collapsing the past into the present, he sought to destabilise the regime by proving that its only achievement had been to make things worse. Nothing is more subversive than the traces of yesteryear, or so Orwell seemed to suggest.

And so it proved. My reading of *Nineteen Eighty-Four* reinforced my tentative adolescent radicalism by fusing it with history. The problem with the anarcho-punk scene was that it was all too grimly contemporary. However much it reflected my crude populism and my need to see things in manichaean terms, its insistence on living in the present unnerved me. I wasn't the sort of boy who could cope with too much black leather or too much ear-splitting noise. What Orwell seemed to do was to take all my prejudices and bathe them in the homely light of the 1940s. His portrait of the 'proles' is a case in point. As I've already tried to show, I'd originally been attracted to working people (and hence to the left) by the absurd belief that they had a genius for shirking their responsibilities. Orwell did precisely nothing to rid me of this delusion. Instead he took the myth of the noble savage and invested it with a peculiarly English charm. I can see in retrospect that what most attracted me to the proles was their instinctive suspicion of reason. It wasn't so much that they didn't work (most of them did – and unimaginably hard) but that they didn't *think*. Towards the end of Part 3, shortly after making love for what turns out to be the last time, Winston and Julia gaze down at a middle-aged washerwoman who is hanging out clothes on a line. It is clear that her responses to the world are almost entirely physical. Possessed of a memorably coarse and porcine body, she seems to react with a sort of immemorial wisdom to the desires, urgencies and ethical promptings that register in her gut. There is no question of her thinking things through or 'using her loaf' – a favourite metaphor of one of my prissier teachers. She knows what to do by instinct alone.

Why would a boy of fifteen find this sort of thing so compelling? One answer is that it was a wonderful antidote to failure. At about this time in school I was doing spectacularly badly in every subject except English. If my own powers of reasoning were so obviously inadequate, it seemed reasonable to suppose that a world of pure instinct was where I belonged. But that was something I'd concluded a long time ago. What made *Nineteen Eighty-Four* different (to make the point for the last time) was its tantalising sense of the past. At some level I must have known that Oceania's proles were a fantasy from a different age. The washerwoman with her 'thick arms' and 'powerful mare-like buttocks' had nothing in common with the gum-chewing girls in Swansea who wore white plastic shoes, drank Babycham by the bucketload and burnt it all off at the gym. Nowhere in the city did grubby men wear mufflers and order a 'pint of wallop' at spit-and-sawdust pubs. But I didn't let that bother me. In a blatant act of doublethink I convinced myself that working people were the same in 1982 as they had been in 1984, if you take my meaning. This made it all the easier to embrace the idea that one day the people would rule. History had seeped into my everyday life and from now on I would live in the past and the present at the same time.

One other thing. In his great essay 'Inside the Whale', Orwell said that when he first read the work of Henry Miller he got the feeling that 'he [Miller] wrote this specially for me'.[11] As has often been pointed out, many people have had precisely the same experience when first reading Orwell. I'm one of them. Right from the start I had the feeling that Orwell was sitting opposite me in a comfortable chair, rolling one of his full-strength cigarettes and genially expounding ideas I didn't

11 George Orwell, 'Inside the Whale' in Peter Davison (ed.), *The Complete Works of George Orwell, Vol. 12: A Patriot After All 1940-1941* (London: Secker and Warburg, 2000), p. 88.

know I had. To this day I can't read a sentence of his work without thinking 'Ah! It's George!' It's something I've thought about a lot over the years. There are times when I'm inclined to interpret it in almost occult terms. If a writer like Orwell has the capacity to anticipate our thoughts, perhaps it's the case that our intellectual development is somehow mapped out in advance. Perhaps our every thought is encoded in our brains and activated in due course by the appropriate stimulus, like a firework that's primed to go off at a dramatic point in a rock concert. Nothing is voluntary. Everything that passes across our minds is dictated by some cosmic Big Brother.

Or perhaps not. The likelier explanation for my sense of kinship with Orwell is much less elevated. When I skipped through *Nineteen Eighty-Four* and concluded that something truly momentous had occurred in my life, I suppose I was suffering from the sort of intellectual arrogance that only afflicts the extremely ignorant. At fifteen my brain was almost wholly unexercised. The only things that had ever interested me were moods, ambiences and feelings. It's true that I sometimes deployed a low-level verbal flair (or what passed for flair in my lousy comprehensive school) to sound off about subjects I'd never bothered to master, but I hadn't made the slightest effort to understand anything difficult or abstract or important. Like Eliot's J. Alfred Prufrock I was 'full of high sentence but a bit obtuse',[12] but at the same time – in sharp contrast to Prufrock – I had no sense at all of my intellectual limitations. My ignorance of what it meant to think, combined with a sense of educational entitlement I'd inherited from my parents, led me to imagine that profound truths could be easily grasped. My early responses to Orwell were not those of a serious reader but of someone who simply gestured towards seriousness. The sense that Orwell was reading my mind – the desire to shout 'Yes – that's it!' after every page – only arose because I *thought* I understood what he said. In reality I understood next to nothing. Faced with a

12 T.S. Eliot, 'The Love Song of J. Alfred Prufrock' in *Collected Poems 1909-1962* (London: Faber and Faber, 1980), p. 17.

pregnant aphorism or an intriguing piece of dialogue or one of Goldstein's dense philosophical meditations, I'd congratulate myself on appreciating its significance before darting off to the next page. The enthusiasm I brought to the text was inversely proportional to the level of my comprehension. The business of thinking would come later.

In the few weeks after reading *Nineteen Eighty-Four* I developed two characteristics that have remained with me to this day. The first was a deeply irritating habit of sharing my knowledge with all and sundry. Bowled over by Orwell's vision of heroism in the face of dictatorship, I started buttonholing friends, relatives and domestic animals and telling them all about it. No detail of Winston's battle with Big Brother was too trivial for me to rehearse at length in hushed and breathless tones. Some members of my audience seemed quite pleased. My parents were so relieved that I'd finally read a serious book (as opposed to overwritten volumes on rock music) that they heard me out in bored politeness. Others were not so delighted. When I summarised the plot for Julian and told him about Winston's agonising reconciliation with the system, he grimaced as if to say 'Too much information!' and shot me a look of deep annoyance. It turned out that he'd also borrowed a copy of *Nineteen Eighty-Four* from his father but had only read the first fifty pages. 'Now that you've told me the end I won't be able to read it until I've forgotten what you said', he moaned. I know for certain that he still hasn't bothered.

The other characteristic I began to acquire was a species of literary obsessiveness. Having decided that Orwell and I were cut from the same cloth I now set out to read all his work. My father surrendered his copy of *Animal Farm* and I bolted it in a single sitting, paralysed by a sense of foreboding when the pigs went up on their hind legs on the last page. Shortly afterwards I bought copies of some of the lesser-known texts from 'Ralph the Books', a secondhand bookshop in the centre of Swansea that had once been haunted by a young Dylan Thomas. Orwell's non-fiction hit me so hard that twenty years later I felt compelled to write a book about it. The spurious feeling that I *really knew* this man was boosted to ludicrous extremes by his writings on tramps, boys' comics and nice cups of tea – all subjects on which I regarded myself as an expert. Yet something began to nag. For a while I'd thought of Orwell as a sort of honorary anarchist, not least because his hatred of the state reminded me so much of Crass. Now I began to realise that he was nothing of the sort. Every time I opened one of his books I seemed to be staring at the word 'Socialism'. At first I resisted the temptation to find out what the word meant, prompted (or so I like to think) by the clairvoyant realisation that to do so would change everything. Then Julian told me that a meeting on anarchism was due to take place at the Central Library on Alexandra Road. It had been organised by the Socialist Party of Great Britain. Did I want to go?

I did. The meeting took place on a Friday evening in the spring of 1982, only a few weeks after the Crass gig on the Sandfields Estate. Julian and I arrived about ten minutes early and were ushered into the Reading Room of the library by a vague-looking pensioner in a tatty blue sweater. As I waited for the talk to begin I sat self-consciously with my hands on my lap and breathed in the ambience. Once again I felt that the membrane between the past and the present had begun to dissolve. The Reading Room seemed as redolent of earlier times as my copy of *Nineteen Eighty-Four*. A sort of late-Victorian municipal seriousness was the medium in which everything moved. The walls were impossibly high and stained yellow with old age, though the impression they conveyed was one of tired grandeur rather than decrepitude. Attached to each of them was a polished mahogany board, inclined at an angle of about fifteen degrees, whose purpose was to display the current crop of newspapers. The librarians had been scrupulously democratic. There was everything from *The Times* and the *Daily Telegraph* on the right to the *Morning Star*, *Soviet Weekly* and *Tribune* on the left. All the papers were held in place by bronze rods that divided them in their centre pages. Looking around at that teeming variety of broadsheets and tabloids with their plethora of headlines, mastheads and typefaces, I was struck for the first time by a sense of the sheer complexity of adult life. All at once I was a citizen of Babel. The world suddenly seemed to consist of a billion urgent voices, each of them blurting out opinions whose only point of similarity was the passion with which they were held. It was a night for revelations. The conversation of mankind had got me in its grip.[13]

The Chairwoman called for silence at about 7.40, a mere ten minutes after the meeting was due to begin. She and the speaker sat behind a magnificent oak table but they were not on a different level to the rest of us. Hierarchies had been temporarily dismantled. Reminding us that his theme was anarchism and that he intended to approach it from a Marxist perspective, the speaker finessed his way into action. I suppose he was the sort of socialist whom Orwell might have been too narrow-minded to appreciate. Grey haired, bespectacled and genial, he came across like a university lecturer who had thrown it all up for a career in market gardening. His shirtleeves, sandals and woollen socks spoke eloquently of the soil. Somehow one envisaged him digging the garden on autumn afternoons and turning up large quantities of potatoes. From time to time he dipped into a pouch of tobacco and made himself a cigarette, pausing to light it between one clause and another. A large 'No Smoking' sign loomed on the wall behind him.

What an orator! Recognising that Julian and I were the only tyros in the audience, he went out of his way to make us feel welcome in the House of Marx. Every so often he glanced over and gave us an avuncular smile, as if to say 'I know it's difficult but stick at it – these are momentous ideas you're hearing!' In actual fact he spoke little enough about anarchism, which he dismissed as a well-meaning but naive ideology whose influence

13 The phrase 'conversation of mankind' was coined by the conservative philosopher Michael Oakeshott in his essay 'The Voice of Poetry in the Conversation of Mankind'. See Oakeshott, *Rationalism in Politics and Other Essays* (London: Methuen, 1981 [1962]) p. 197f.

on young people was a matter of regret. His real subject was the beautiful dream of International Socialism. He told us that the ills of the world were largely due to something called 'capitalism', whose lust for profit engendered wars, poverty and ruined lives in equal measure. The good news was that History had instructed the working class to destroy the system forever. In the future we would live in a world in which the 'means of production' (o thou most resonant of phrases!) would be owned by everyone. There would be no need for the market and each of us would take whatever he needed from the communal stores. Alienation, ugliness and the fraught distinction between 'us' and 'them' would simply disappear. The age of universal creativity would at last be upon us.

I understood about a third of it but in my heart I embraced it all. During the round of applause at the end of the talk I beamed like a child at the circus. The speaker caught sight of me, suppressed an astonished laugh and mouthed the words 'thank you'.[14] And then came another new experience. The Chairwoman told us that the thirty or so minutes until nine o' clock would be taken up with questions and answers. As I twisted in my seat to get a glimpse of each questioner, I didn't realise that I'd embarked on an ethnographic quest that would fascinate me for many years to come. For good or ill I'd begun to classify the types (or is that stereotypes?) who populate socialist meetings and speak from the floor.

First off the mark was an exotic looking man in his late thirties with a luxuriant moustache and a mass of black curls. Introducing himself as the Secretary of the SPGB's Swansea Branch, he complimented the speaker on his talk and treated us to a display of extreme fluency. He told us that a colleague of his at the university had recently claimed that people weren't

14 After reading the manuscript of this book, Howard Moss – a leading member of the SPGB and a fine orator in his own right – delved into his personal archive and discovered that the speaker I describe here was Ron Cook (1927-2008). For a brief obituary of Cook, see *Socialist Standard*, No. 1246, June 2008. Towards the end of his life, Cook sketched his vision of socialism in a stimulating self-published book entitled *Yes – Utopia!* (West Bromwich. 2003). I honour his memory.

good enough to make a go of socialism. It was important to understand why this wasn't true: 'When people tell us that socialism is contrary to human nature', or so he continued, 'they always assume that it's got something to do with self-sacrifice. It hasn't. Socialism isn't about the denial of our needs but about their realisation. I don't want socialism for everyone else. I want it for myself.' With the benefit of hindsight I suspect that this rousing statement of revolutionary egoism had been inspired by Oscar Wilde. At any rate the questioner's type was clear. He was the bookish lecturer with the silver tongue and the panoramic knowledge of intellectual history. I still learn something interesting every time I talk to him.

The other contribution that sticks in my mind came from someone who was rather more *sui generis*. Sitting near the door was a short woman in extreme old age who nursed a packet of ten Benson and Hedges. One could tell from her arched back, her cheap nylon sweater and her ash-grey hair that she'd spent much of her life never quite earning enough. What was distinctive about her was her combination of innocence and sincerity. Almost alone among the Marxists I've known she eschewed the empire of theory. Everything boiled down to a few divine simplicities. She told us that when she'd last been to London, not so many years ago, she'd seen tramps sleeping on benches in full view of Buckingham Palace. The contrast between poverty and plenty was seared in her memory. How wonderful to know that everything would be different in the future: 'Under socialism we'll share and share alike and no one will be in need.' It was a childlike but curiously powerful intervention. Her voice and her hands trembled with emotion as she uttered her final words. A con vert of no more than an hour, I nodded my head vigorously as she resumed her seat.

Naturally I asked a question and naturally it made no sense. The speaker responded to it with exquisite politeness. Then the meeting was formally closed and Julian and I made our way home. In my hands I held a copy of that month's *Socialist Standard* and a pamphlet entitled *Is a Third World War Inevitable?*, the first socialist publications I had ever bought. Something strange had happened to my sense of space. Throughout his talk the speaker had alluded briefly and expertly to a torrent of different places – Washington, London, Leningrad, Bombay, Santiago and virtually everywhere else. His peripatetic rhetoric had widened and vivified my field of vision in a way that was slowly building to a climax. For a few delirious hours I sensed the presence of what Ouspensky might have called 'horizons infinitely remote and incredibly beautiful'.[15] The whole world seemed to converge on my gaze. As Julian and I chattered our way up Constitution Hill and through the network of streets above the city, I somehow felt connected to the boulevards of Europe and the parched fields of India and the snowy expanses of the Arctic. The distinction between 'here' and 'there' had all but disappeared. My spirit settled like a light mist across every last inch of the planet, sucking up knowledge and a new sense of purpose.

The feelings peaked as Julian and I approached the border of Cwmdonkin Park, another of Dylan Thomas's old haunts. After climbing the fence that divided the park from the large derelict house standing next to it, I looked out at the perfectly tended lawns, the picturesque shelters and the ornamental gardens as they glimmered in the moonlight. A great arc of excitement expanded across my chest. There is no way of describing what I saw. It seemed as if an inexhaustible supply of phosphorescent energy was burning beneath the surface of the earth, bringing strength, unity and power to everything that it touched. The universe palpitated with significance. For a few moments the *élan vital* and I were in intimate communication.

I'm not mad. I know that my experiences that night were the product of my overheated imagination, not a revelation of some deeper reality. But a certain grandiloquence goes with the territory. My first exposure to the Marxist passion play had acted on my nervous system like manna from heaven. When I woke up the following morning I realised that something

15 Quoted in Colin Wilson, *The Occult* (London: Grafton, 1989), p. 48.

decisive had happened. My habit of dividing the world into endless forbidding vistas and tiny spaces of refuge had somehow disappeared. The manichaean curse had been lifted. Still invigorated by the speaker's unforgettable display of global consciousness – still thrilled beyond measure by his sublime confidence that freedom would one day exist everywhere – I began to conceive of every last acre of the planet as somewhere where the spirit could find sustenance. Things would be different now. The world had suddenly become bigger.

I never joined the SPGB and I gave up attending its meetings after a year or so, but I was fortunate that it provided me with my introduction to the left. I still regard it as the most principled and certainly the most loveable of all the Marxist sects in Britain. In many respects it set a standard of political integrity by which I've judged all the other socialist parties. The only problem was that its enormous strengths ultimately derived from its equally enormous weaknesses – weaknesses which made it wholly ineffective as an organ of political change. Let me try and draw out the paradox.

The SPGB was established in 1904 at a conference in the Printers' Hall near Fleet Street.[16] Its founders were a group of so-called 'Impossibilists' who had been expelled from H. M. Hyndman's Social Democratic Federation (SDF), the first Marxist organisation in Britain. At the heart of their politics was a brutally uncompromising attitude towards the issue of 'reformism'. The SDF had always campaigned for 'immediate reforms' of the capitalist system, on the grounds that they would pave the way for full-blooded socialism. The Impossibilists thought of immediate reforms as the work of the bourgeois Devil. If activists were sidetracked into demanding a better electoral system or a new poor law or the nationalisation of this or that, it followed that they would soon lose sight of the socialist Valhalla and content themselves with a few more scraps

16 For the history of the SPGB, see Robert Barltrop, *The Monument: The Story of the Socialist Party of Great Britain* (London: Pluto Press, 1975).

from the capitalist table. The purpose of a socialist party was not to mess around in the shallows of bourgeois politics. Its goal was the creation of a new world. This could only be achieved by explaining what was wrong with capitalism and projecting the socialist alternative.

All roads lead to 1904. The SPGB has hardly altered its politics in over a century, and its hostility to reformism tells us everything we need to know about its failures and its victories. Let us begin with the failures. Here's how I once heard them described by an old-fashioned communist debater at Hyde Park Corner, serving up tired aphorisms and worldly condescension on a chilly winter afternoon: 'The sad truth is that socialism cannot be made by propaganda alone. Persuading people of the need for change is an agonisingly incremental process. If the left confines itself to pointing the way to utopia, only a handful of impressionable motorists will speed off in the right direction. What socialists have to do is to prove their mettle in the everyday world. A single successful reform is worth more than a thousand pamphlets. By legislating to improve people's lives in the here and now, a radical left government can begin to shift society towards fundamental change. Otherwise there is no hope. It was the SPGB's failure to grasp this point which consigned it to the wilderness. It has never had more than 500 members.'

Quite so. Yet in a curious way the Impossibilists were proved right. While other organisations mired themselves in workaday politics and its grubby compromises, the SPGB kept its eyes firmly on the millennium. Its biggest achievement was to tend the flame of utopia when others were deserting it. In over 30 years I have never heard a discussion of socialism at a meeting of the Communist Party. At meetings of the SPGB I scarcely heard anything else. Nearly all its orators were as thrillingly messianic as that first speaker at the Central Library, conjuring a world in which money, the state and the market had been abolished forever. Nor was their impact purely rhetorical. By the force of their rhetoric they ennobled the character of their listeners, if only for a few hours at a time. Left to marinate in what Michael Foot has called 'the purest milk of the word',[17] everyone behaved as if the good society had already arrived. Comradely courtesies were always the rule and never the exception. Different views were listened to respectfully and debated rationally. Love was exchanged for love and trust for trust.[18] On the first page of William Morris's *News from Nowhere*, one of the books which Impossibilist orators referred to continually, a world-weary activist yearns for a glimpse of what socialism might be like: 'If I could but see it! If I could but see it!'[19] All those years ago, in a handful of ill-attended meetings in a small provincial library, I like to think that I *did* see it.

But what was I looking at, exactly? In a sense I saw the past as much as the future. The SPGB was the oldest Marxist organisation in Britain, outstripping its nearest rival by a good sixteen years, and it took its responsibilities to history very seriously. Somehow or other its members had preserved the ethos of late-Victorian and Edwardian radicalism. Their sense of what socialism might *feel like* was clearly derived from the work of Morris, Walter Crane and Edward Carpenter. You only have to glance at some of Crane's utopian etchings to understand what I mean. In most of them the socialist future is not depicted as urban, industrial or secular but as bucolic and vaguely mystical. The landscape is fertile, green and strewn with flowers. The atmosphere is defined by crystalline light and soft breezes. None of the willowy beauties who drift from place to place is afflicted by hunger or desire. Their strange Botticellian faces survey the world from afar, registering great calm but no hint of 'I want'. Their clothes are loose and flowing and their limbs are miraculously supple. I won't say that my friends in the

17 Michael Foot, *Debts of Honour* (London: Picador, 1980), p. 109.

18 'If we assume *man* to be *man*, and his relation to the world to be a human one, then love can only be exchanged for love, trust for trust, and so on.' See Karl Marx, 'Economic and Philosophical Manuscripts' in *Early Writings*, edited by Lucio Colletti (Harmondsworth: Pelican, 1975), p. 379.

19 William Morris, *Selected Writings and Designs*, edited by Asa Briggs (Harmondsworth: Pelican, 1968), p. 184.

Central Library captured their mood exactly, but it was clearly what they aspired to. Even the poorest and oldest of them seemed to be striving, sometimes with a cheerful expectation of failure, to live up to an ideal that had been sketched out more than a century earlier. Orwell had taught me that history could seep into the present. The SPGB reinforced my desire to live in it.

I have one other reason to be grateful to the SPGB. Its attitude towards politics was a wonderful prophylactic against all kinds of ultra-leftist nonsense. Not all the Marxist parties in Britain can be relied upon to take democracy seriously, though they cry foul quickly enough when their own rights are violated. The SPGB was different. Its members worshipped democracy with a touching and unembarrassed ardour. They seemed to regard a vigorous clash of opinions as a panacea for all human ills. If they took exception to what another party or organisation had said (and in practice they disagreed with virtually everyone), their instinct was to challenge one of its members to a public debate. These events were renowned among connoisseurs of fringe politics for their astonishing displays of dialectical virtuosity. More than a few senior politicians have been holed below the waterline by the SPGB's ragged trousered polemicists, whose political high explosives were always theatrical as well as intellectual. One of the party's greatest debaters, the legendary Tony Turner, allegedly made a habit of eating fruit from a paper bag while listening to his opponents. His favourite tactic was to pop a cherry into his mouth, gorge noisily on the flesh and then spit out the stone in an unanswerable display of political contempt. No one ever defeated him. These days he'd probably fall foul of the health-and-safety laws. Cherries can be dangerous, after all.

There was nothing inconsistent about the SPGB's take on democracy. Its hunger for free speech pervaded everything it said and did. Its disdain for the countries of 'actually existing socialism' was bracingly immoderate. China, Russia, Cuba and the 'people's democracies' of Eastern Europe were witheringly dismissed as 'state-capitalist' frauds. The idea that a socialist party ought to have leaders was scorned to high heaven. And best of all there was a burning faith in the power of free elections. I still have a vivid recollection of Stephen Coleman, now a celebrated political scientist, stroking his vast beard and telling his Swansea audience that 'Working people can establish a socialist society by voting for it at the ballot box'. I knew at once that this was one of the truths I'd cherish for the rest of my life. Thanks to the SPGB I've been a parliamentary socialist since the age of fifteen, and I see no reason to apologise for it. Soviet power? No thanks.[20]

Everyone knows that Marxist organisations tend to multiply like amoeba. Every year or so a no-holds-barred ideological row will divide one party or another down the middle, causing a small but deeply embittered faction to break away and found a party of its own. For people who disdain the rhetoric of *laissez-faire* capitalism, Marxists have an enormous talent for littering the political market with a wide choice of goods. Today there are twenty or so organisations in Britain which regard themselves as vanguard parties of the working class. In my younger days there were even more. As I began to move away from the SPGB, thrilled by its internal culture but dismayed by its lack of activism, I flirted with quite a few of them. For a period of about eighteen months, roughly between the summer of 1982 and the start of the Miners' Strike in 1984, I toured the byways of the left with little more than slogans, enthusiasm and chutzpah to keep me going. If nothing else I received a world-class education in political eccentricity.

What I didn't receive was much of an intellectual boost. At this stage I still suffered from the delusions of intellectual grandeur that had marred my reading of Orwell. Believing that Marxism could be reduced to a few clichés about class struggle, the crisis

20 To be precise, I tend to agree with Nicos Poulantzas that a socialist society should seek to allow soviets and national parliaments to co-exist in some sort of creative tension. But that is a subject for another occasion.

of capitalism and the need for workers' control, I thought I grasped everything when in fact I understood nothing. The result was that my political engagements were conducted more at the level of aesthetics than of ideology. As I moved around restlessly from group to group, scanning a newspaper here and attending a meeting there, I acquired a basic knowledge of their political programmes but never anything more. My real focus was on their distinctive habits of mind and body, or what Pierre Bourdieu might have called their 'habitus'. The more I saw of the various socialist parties (and no teenager ever shopped on the left as enthusiastically as I did), the more I discovered about their tastes, their emotional capacities and their ways of seeing. It became clear that the world of the Marxist sects was insuperably divided by vast differences of *character*. The sort of person who joined the Socialist Workers Party bore no resemblance to the sort of person who joined the International Marxist Group or the Workers' Revolutionary Party. The stereotypical 'Marxist subversive' was evidently a media fiction.

In the early 1980s the most prominent Marxist organisation in Swansea was a Trotskyist outfit called the Militant Tendency, whose members sold their newspaper outside Marks and Spencer on Saturday mornings.[21] Most people referred to it simply as 'Militant'. It had been founded in 1964 and practised the tactic of 'entryism', which meant that it operated inside the Labour Party and tried to spread its message among the party's grass roots. The 1980s was its one period of significant influence. Among other things it gained control of Liverpool City Council, saw three of its members elected to parliament (all in the Labour interest) and played a decisive role in the campaign against the Poll Tax. I stick to the unfashionable belief that Militant did a great deal more good than harm. It had a particularly strong following in the Swansea West constituency, where its members

21 For the history of the Militant Tendency, see Michael Crick, *Militant* (London: Faber and Faber, 1984); John Callaghan, *British Trotskyism: Theory and Practice* (London: Blackwell, 1984), Chapter 7. See also Alan Woods, *Ted Grant: The Permanent Revolutionary* (London: Wellred, 2013).

made persistent attempts to replace the sitting MP, a slightly colourless right winger called Alan Williams, with a candidate of their own called Alec Thraves. The contrast between the two men could scarcely have been greater. Thraves was a talented activist with a resonant Swansea accent and a deep cauldron of proletarian sincerity. Williams had an Oxford degree, a condescending manner and an undeniable gift for concision. On one occasion they were both interviewed about Welsh politics for a programme on the BBC. After Thraves rattled off a highly attractive but not entirely practical list of 'socialist policies', insisting that a Labour government should strive to implement them in its first term, Williams smiled sardonically and said 'The nice thing about Alec is the way he tells them.' Never had the difference betwen the ardent idealism of the Labour left and the flippant *hauteur* of the Croslandite right been thrown into more vivid relief.

Militant often complained that it was misrepresented by the media. In a way it was right. More or less the only member who ever appeared on television was Derek Hatton, a cocky little wide boy who served as Deputy Leader of Liverpool City Council for a couple of years. With his preposterously sharp suits, laddish football references and hunger for self-advancement, Hatton had virtually nothing in common with the other members of Militant. The organisation's house style was what we used to call 'workerist', though sometimes with an interesting twist. Like many people who called themselves Marxists, Militant supporters had clearly been traumatised by post-war changes in working-class culture. They detested the consumer paradise that allowed mechanics or shop assistants to visit glitzy night clubs, drink foreign lager and wear flashy off-the-peg clothes. In response they fell back on the most primitive archetypes of industrial labour. When they gathered on the streets, holding their newspapers in front of their chests and shouting slogans like 'Labour to power on a socialist programme', they looked as if they'd just finished a twenty-hour shift at the ironworks. Brooding machismo defiance and a sort of self-regarding dowdiness were the order of the day. Flat caps, cheap bomber jackets and sturdy brown shoes reflected an extreme austerity of spirit. Their oratory was a legend in itself. I once went to the Swansea leisure centre to attend a regional conference of the Labour Party Young Socialists, an organisation which Militant dominated. It soon became clear that the discussion of politics was not on the agenda. The sole purpose of the event was to shower teenage activists in the higher Trotskyist uplift. Assiduously dropping every 'h' in the book, Militant speakers in drip-dry nylon shirts told us to 'old our 'eads 'igh for resisting Tory cuts. Swearing was strictly forbidden. When I used the word 'fuck' in a conversation with a 'leading comrade' from Llanelli, he told me that 'You'll never win over the workers with language like that.' For some reason I still feel slightly contrite about it.

Members of Militant were rarely given to introspection, so I don't suppose many of them ever thought too deeply about the image they projected. If a quick-thinking activist had been asked to justify it, he would probably have done so on utilitarian grounds: 'The struggle for human liberation is long and hard, comrade. Revolutionaries shouldn't be distracted by fripperies.' But there was more to it than that. As I've said, Militant's inveterate workerism often came with a twist. From time to time the flat caps, bomber jackets and sturdy shoes were accompanied by something a bit more contemporary and a bit more (how can I put this?) sexual. One of the Swansea contingent had his hair cut in the same style as a member of Duran Duran – quiffed on the top, shaved at the sides and long at the back. Another wore a pink scarf. Some of them – often the most defiantly working class in terms of their speech and body language – sometimes wore jeans so tight that they looked as if they'd donated their testicles to the Militant Fighting Fund. I suspect these stylistic inconsistencies were evidence of a deep psychological conflict. However much they hated the cheap sexual glitter of the consumer age, many members of Militant were also secretly attracted to it. Desperate to overcome their guilt, they adopted a brutally ascetic style in order to keep their inner hedonist at bay. The caricature proletarians who gathered outside Marks and Spencer on Saturdays weren't simply paying tribute to the power of the working class. Some of them were fighting a losing battle against the siren voices of desire.

I could go further. In his novel *Redemption* (1990), a sharp satire on modern Trotskyism, Tariq Ali has a character called Jed Burroughs. Burroughs is transparently based on Ted Grant, the indefatigable South African who founded Militant and served as its de facto leader until it left the Labour Party in the early 1990s. Ali makes it perfectly clear that Burroughs (and by implication his real-life model) is a repressed homosexual of the most anguished kind. Too ashamed to admit to his longings and always wearing a 'dirty grey raincoat',[22] he limits his private life to seeking 'instant gratification' in 'certain public lavatories'.[23] His politics are merely an indirect expression of his tortured libido. His only means of sublimating his sexuality is to impose an iron discipline on the organisation he leads, which Ali somewhat archly refers to as the 'Burrowers League'. There is nothing homophobic about Ali's characterisation. His point is a straightforwardly liberationist one: If people try to suppress their deepest desires, or so he seems to tell us, their souls will slowly be colonised by misery, frustration and seediness.[24]

I'm not suggesting that everyone in Militant had the same problems as Jed Burroughs. Most of them were fairly stable, in an ideologically dubious sort of way. But everyone on the left has a tale to tell about an encounter with a Militant weirdo. Here's mine. One day in 1987 (I remember the year because the General Election was in full swing) I was travelling between London and Swansea on the train. A member of Militant got

22 Tariq Ali, *Redemption* (London: Chatto and Windus, 1990), p. 118.

23 Ibid., p. 124.

24 I had better put on record my belief that Ali was being grossly unfair to Grant, whose contribution to the history of the British left was stimulating, honourable and worth remembering. Two of Grant's most interesting followers – Alan Woods and Rob Sewell – came from Swansea and went on to found the International Marxist Tendency (IMT).

on at Bridgend, sat opposite me and glanced at the cover of the book I was reading. Seeing that it was a copy of *The British Economic Disaster* by Andrew Glyn and John Harrison, two of Militant's leading thinkers, he launched into an unstoppable cascade of chat. He was probably the most egotistical Marxist I have ever met. For nearly an hour he portrayed himself as a sort of Zelig of the revolutionary left. He claimed to have manned the picket lines at Saltley Gate, Grunwick and Orgreave and to have battled the police at all of them. At one point he even rolled up his sleeve to show me a nasty mark on his forearm, allegedly the result of a 'major altercation' at Wapping. I dare say he got it after falling off a bike.

Then something extraordinary happened. My boastful Trotskyist glanced furtively around the carriage, leaned in close like a practised conspirator and asked 'Are you not nice?' His sallow features betrayed a strange combination of fear, embarrassment and excitement. I was too naive to understand what he was talking about, though it crossed my mind that he was was asking me whether I was a homosexual. I asked him to repeat the question and he immediately slumped back in his seat, waving his hand in front of his face as if to say 'It doesn't matter'. Little more was said in the few minutes before we reached Swansea. A couple of days later I ran into a gay friend of mine, who confirmed that 'not nice' was indeed a euphemism for what he grinningly called 'membership of the faith'. Part of me was slightly taken aback. I didn't mind that the guy from Militant had tried to seduce me, only that he'd prepared the ground with such a preening display of macho nonsense. It seemed a shame that he could only affirm his sexuality after trying to disavow it. Here at least his militancy had failed him.

Two other Trotskyist organisations had a presence in Swansea in the early 1980s. The first was the Socialist Workers Party (SWP), which appealed heavily to students and whose theoretical guru, the bumptious but affable Tony Cliff, spoke regularly in the city over a period of thirty years.[25] I once heard Cliff tell a student who arrived late at a meeting that she would 'miss the train to the Finland Station'. To the very end he seemed to believe that he was destined to be the British Lenin, yet for all his pretensions his influence was a largely constructive one. His extreme hatred of the Soviet Union and the other socialist countries, which he echoed the SPGB in calling 'state capitalist', reminded several generations of young activists that socialism cannot be built in the absence of democracy. His politics were summed up in the rather stirring slogan 'Neither Washington nor Moscow but International Socialism'. One afternoon in school I scrawled it on the cover of an exercise book and was immediately sent to detention by my English teacher. Free speech is a wonderful thing.

I think it's fair to say that the Swansea Branch of the SWP was quite different from its counterparts elsewhere in the country. For one thing its leading members had their roots in anarchism rather than Marxism. Many of them had cut their teeth in an anarchist subculture that flared spectacularly in Swansea in the 1970s, achieved a number of improbable successes and then dwindled almost to nothing. (It had all but died out by the time of the anarcho-punk scene.) Under the incendiary leadership of Ian Bone, who later moved to London and founded the Class War movement, the Swansea anarchists produced a paper called *Alarm* which accused leading councillors of financial corruption. The result was that the Labour Party briefly lost control of the city and several members of the 'Swansea Mafia' went to jail.[26] The activists who went over to the SWP had a very recognisable style. Theirs was a world of beards, languor and trips to the dole office. Oblivious to Tony Cliff's emphasis on industrial struggle, they had all resigned their jobs and devoted

25 For the history of the SWP, see Callaghan, *British Trotskyism*, Chapter 5. Cf. Tony Cliff, *A World to Win: Life of a Revolutionary* (London: Bookmarks, 2000).

26 For a fascinating account of the anarchist movement in Swansea in the 1970s, see Ian Bone, *Bash the Rich: True-Life Confessions of an Anarchist in the UK* (Bath: Tangent Books, 2006).

themselves to a life of leisurely subversion. Their antipathy to the Protestant work ethic was awesome in its scale. Whenever they appeared on the streets to sell *Socialist Worker*, usually outside a plate-glass shopping complex called the Quadrant, they came across like weary opium-eaters on the verge of blissful sleep. If anyone asked for a paper they would delay handing it over by at least thirty seconds, pausing instead to finish a conversation, light a cigarette or simply watch a blackbird streaking across the sky. At this time in South Wales there were thousands of people on the dole. The narcoleptic sages of the SWP sympathised with them all and showed no understanding of their predicament. Like the anarchists they had once been, their real interest was in the right *not* to work.

The inevitable consequence of the SWP's torpor was a woeful lack of political effectiveness. One member in particular had a reputation throughout Swansea as the most maladroit activist in Western Christendom. His name was Dan and his beard was so bushy it often preceded him around corners. Apparently he was quite a talented mathematician and had worked for a few years as a lecturer in the local university, only to suffer a nervous breakdown in his late twenties. Ever since then he'd been subsisting on invalidity benefit and putting the case for the SWP at every public meeting in the city. His celebrated interventions were clearly fuelled by a deep sense of shame. Aware that people were calling him a sponger and a bludger behind his back, Dan would get to his feet and transform himself into a whirling dervish of self-justification. Gesticulating wildly and firing off little missiles of spit from the corners of his mouth, he always portrayed himself as a master strategist in the ongoing struggle for social justice. At first he was relatively restrained and articulate, seeking to win our approval by peddling anecdotes about leading members of the Labour Movement: 'I was proud to be arrested with Arthur Scargill at Grunwick in 1977'. Then his tongue would get the better of him and little yelps of discomfort would punctuate every sentence. Anecdotes, statistics and slogans began to slop around in an indigestible mush. The SWP was all but forgotten and the pronoun 'I' was deployed far too frequently for comfort. By the time he sat down the sound of suppressed laughter hovered like sulphur. No one was ever converted. After one extravaganza an elderly comrade turned to face me, raised his eyes to the heavens and said 'Nice chap, Dan. Can't speak in public to save his fucking life'. I had never heard him swear before.[27]

And then there was Lucy – the magnificent, extravagantly gifted, fated Lucy. Lucy was a leading member of the youth wing of the International Marxist Group (IMG), the other Trotskyist organisation with a following in Swansea.[28] When I first met her she was standing outside the Odeon cinema on the Kingsway, trying to sell copies of *Revolution* to a comically indifferent public. It was 1982 but she had taken her sartorial cues from the student radicals of 1968. Her boyish figure was bundled up in a pair of khaki trousers, a threadbare plaid jacket and the sort of roll-necked sweater that Michel Foucault used to wear. Her irresistibly puckish face beamed out at the world from beneath a ludicrous red beret. I had never encountered such lightness of spirit in anyone who called herself a Marxist. Every time some graceless member of the public refused to buy her paper, she said 'thank you' in a cut-glass accent, turned smartly on her heels and giggled like a debutante after three glasses of champagne. Her eyes sparkled with good humour. How on earth could such charm, eccentricity and seriousness have been combined in the same person?

I never really found out. Lucy was a year or two older than me and too formidable to get to know well, though occasionally I heard about her on the grapevine. It turned out that she was something of a prodigy. The daughter of Italian parents whose respective families had fled to South Wales while Mussolini was doing his worst, she attended a local comprehensive school and terrified the teachers with her precociousness. Even at the age

27 It is only fair to point out that the Swansea branch of the SWP is much more effective now than it was then.

28 For the history of the IMG, see Callaghan, *British Trotskyism*, Chapter 6.

of sixteen she was writing erudite articles on the Middle East for *Revolution*, briskly condemning Islamist groups one had never heard of for their 'petty bourgeois' deviations. Later on she turned down a place at Cambridge on the grounds that the entire university was tainted by elitism. Naturally she got a brilliant First elsewhere. Then she moved to London and led a slightly disjointed life, dividing her time between Trotskyist intrigue and caring for the disabled activist with whom she had fallen in love. Her friends told me that she was happy and I was glad to hear it.

Everyone was certain that Lucy would make a name for herself. Towards the end of the millennium our predictions began to come true. At a meeting in 1999 I bumped into a mutual friend who told me that Lucy had renounced Marxism, taken up a place at Cambridge (irony of ironies) and was studying for a doctorate in Child Psychology. By all accounts her gift with disturbed children was astounding. She could take a rowdy infant Caliban and transform him into a sweet-tempered Ariel with preternatural ease, inspiring envy and admiration in equal measure. One envisaged her squatting on the nursery floor and engaging some nasty little tyke in conversation, winning his trust with her batty smile, an endless fund of stories and a massive bag of sweets. Some of her friends resented the fact that she had given up on the IMG, but I always felt that her new life was not so very different from the old one. The IMG had always put its faith in society's most disenfranchised groups, insisting that women, Third-World revolutionaries and even students were the new source of revolutionary hope. When Lucy devoted her life to some of the most damaged children in Britain, she was simply doing what the IMG had always taught her to do. She was setting aside prejudice, thinking for herself and teasing out the goodness in people whom everyone else wrote off. There was something rather magnificent about it.

If the world were fairer than it is, Lucy's story would have a happy ending. Unfortunately it doesn't. Shortly after turning forty I called in to see Julian, whom I hadn't seen for a couple of months, and we started a long, maudlin and slightly bitchy conversation about the fate of our contemporaries. It struck me that I hadn't heard anything about Lucy for a while, so when I got home I entered her name in Google. The first entry announced that she had 'passed away' about eighteen months previously, less than a year after her partner had died of bronchial pneumonia. The implication was that she hadn't been able to cope with losing the love of her life. I have rarely been so shocked by the death of someone I scarcely knew. For a few days I felt overwhelmed by melancholy. Anxious to make sense of it all, unwilling to believe that the death of someone so gifted had no social meaning, I began to think that Lucy's demise was somehow related to her time in the IMG. Perhaps the collapse of her political faith had affected her more than anyone knew, or so I surmised. Perhaps the triumph of the free market, the disappearance of the Soviet Union and the advent of globalisation had robbed her of her humour, leaving her more than usually vulnerable to traumas in her private life. Perhaps poor, gifted Lucy was yet another victim of the postmodern condition.

My mistake was to make these thoughts public. One evening in an almost empty bar I shared my theory with one of Lucy's old schoolfriends, whose own progress through the IMG had left her disillusioned with politics for life. Her response was pitch perfect: 'Listen, clever-clogs. Lucy loved individuals. She didn't love abstractions. To imply that she died for Trotskyism is to insult her memory.' Then she drained her glass and walked out, pointedly omitting to say goodbye. It was like a bad scene in a novel by Dashiell Hammett. I felt no inclination to go after her.

CHAPTER 4
Requiem for the Miners

In the spring of 2004 at least three meetings were held in Swansea to mark the twentieth anniversary of the outbreak of the Miners' Strike. The best was organised by the Swansea Trades Council and took place in a plush room at the Dolphin Hotel, not a location one usually associates with left-wing activism. The opening speech still sticks in my mind. It was delivered by an elderly woman called Ethel who had travelled down from Merthyr to share her memories of the age of Scargill. In her pink velvet jacket and black corduroy cap she looked more like a character in a soap opera than a tribune of the working class, but her commitment to what she called 'the lads and lasses of the mining communities' was clear as soon as she opened her mouth. Speaking in a one-note nasal drone that sounded more Irish than Welsh, she recalled how the strike had changed her outlook forever. Before it began she had never had a political thought in her life. Within a fortnight of the mines falling silent she had transformed herself into a tireless and efficient activist, organising soup kitchens and ensuring that none of the miners in her area went hungry. Her speech was full of evocative details about getting up in the middle of the night, ferrying food to the picket lines in the freezing mornings and organising Christmas festivities for the miners' children. Memories came flooding back. Even the most cynical among us felt that here was the culture of the Labour Movement at its compassionate best.

And then came the peroration. Having thanked us for listening, Ethel contorted her pleasant grandmother's features into a look signifying 'righteous class anger' and blurted out the following: 'In Merthyr we never had no scabs. Only one man broke the strike and the whole community united against him. To this day he's still refused admission to the local clubs. When he wanted to get married he had to book a hall over thirty miles away. In Merthyr we know what solidarity is all about.'

It was a horribly ungenerous moment. I trust I wasn't the only member of the audience who wanted to shout 'you stupid bitch!' and storm out. Yet in a way the speech would have been incomplete without it. What Ethel had done, emoting her way through her none-too-grammatical recollections, was to exemplify the extraordinary contradictions at the heart of the strike. She was not alone in having her life transformed by the experience of the 'struggle'. Thousands of people, many of whom had never set foot in a mining community, suddenly felt that new possibilities were opening up – possibilities that were as much personal as political, as much to do with the human spirit as with the sombre realities of economics. It was a time for transcending limitations and starting life afresh. At the same time there was a dreadful mood of illiberality in the air. People on both sides of the dispute behaved like intransigent pachyderms, refusing to accept that their ideas were anything less than definitive. Those of us who supported the miners knew perfectly well that there were things we couldn't say. We couldn't say that Arthur Scargill and the rest of the NUM leadership was too inflexible, nor that too many miners were being too violent too often. The idea that a compromise solution might be more realistic than an outright victory was totally *infra dig.* Feelings of sweet liberation alternated with a pervasive sense of despair. The obvious cliché is hard to avoid: It was the best of times and the worst of times.

My own memories of the Miners' Strike reflect these contradictions very clearly. I had just turned seventeen when the strike broke out and had been calling myself a Marxist for about two years. Under its influence I at last became a tolerably serious human being. I began to attend meetings of the Communist Party, made friends with some of the most principled activists in South Wales and immersed myself in the Marxist classics. I'll delay telling you about that until the next chapter. What I want to discuss here is the darker side of the strike. Right from the start I had a slightly jaundiced attitude towards my own side. As sincerely as I backed the miners (and I never seriously doubted that their case was a strong one), I bristled at their demand for unconditional support. I knew from the books I'd begun to read that the British Labour Movement was a magnificently cantankerous beast, no more capable of eschewing debate than of taking a pledge of sobriety. It seemed absurd that we were now being told to support everything the NUM did or bugger off. For the entire twelve months of the strike I held my tongue and hoped for the best. The lesson I learned was that every political movement needs its nay-sayers. Even when the enemy is at the door and the forces of righteousness are running out of ammunition, there must always be room for the unclubbable loner who clings to the margins, questions the majority verdict on principle and demands to have his say. I do not claim that I have always played this role skilfully or wisely (and I'm aware that phrases like 'unclubbable loner' betray a fatal measure of self-regard), but ever since the miners' humiliating defeat I've made a point of saying 'Hang on a minute, comrades' whenever I can. If previously I'd been a squatter in the House of Marx, Arthur Scargill's intransigence turned me into a liberal irritant in one of its ante-rooms – mouthy, carping, wilfully unorthodox. I don't regret it as much as I should.

Many left-wingers in South Wales still cherish a comforting little myth about the origins of the Miners' Strike. It goes something like this. The first few days of March 1984 witnessed the Welsh coalfield's last ever display of mass solidarity. As soon as it became clear that the National Coal Board intended to shut six 'uneconomic' pits in Yorkshire and Scotland, every militant miner at Abernant, Merthyr Vale or Cynheidre realised what was at stake. This was no ordinary attempt to rationalise the mining industry. This was the opening gambit in a ruthless and premeditated campaign to destroy Britain's coalfields, humiliate the NUM and cripple the Labour Movement as a whole. Resistance was a moral necessity. The Welsh miners rose like lions after slumber,[29] immediately starting a 'rock solid' strike that lasted for twelve heroic months. Their eventual defeat had nothing to do with their leaders and everything to do with the brutality of the government, whose police force literally beat them into submission. The struggle will be remembered forever and ever, amen.

Would that it had been so! Things felt very different at the time. Everyone knew that something serious was underway, but the mood in those early days was more one of private doubt than of collective resolve. It was far from clear that the strike had been launched on a solid foundation. In the first three weeks of March I spoke to a number of hardened activists, several of whom expressed the concern, strictly *sotto voce*, that not enough miners seemed genuinely interested in striking. There was particular anxiety about the failure of the NUM's leaders to hold a national ballot. Denied the right to have a say in the most important decision of their lives, many miners felt morally entitled to remain in work or at least to make it clear that they were striking under protest. Unity was absent from the start.

In South Wales the expected surge of militancy never in fact took place. At the time there were 28 pits in the region, all of which have now been closed. The uncomfortable truth is that the workforce only voted to strike in ten of them. All the rest had to be 'picketed out' by militants. Watching these events on television taught me a salutary lesson about a certain type of left-wing mentality. Most of the militants were decent and honourable men, anxious to protect their industry against what they loved to call 'government butchery'. Their one drawback was their curious understanding of democracy. Asked to justify their decision to ignore the views of the majority, they

29 The reference here is to the closing stanza of Shelley's *The Masque of Anarchy* (1819), a left-wing favourite that was much quoted during the strike: 'Rise like lions after slumber/In unvanquishable number/Shake your chains to earth like dew/Which in sleep had fallen on you/Ye are many – they are few.'

immediately resorted to a species of plebeian *amour propre.* 'We have bigger hearts than anyone else', or so they seemed to say. 'Don't you realise how much we love our communities, our jobs, our way of life? Our grandfathers slogged in the pits and our children have the right to do so too. If we don't strike now we sell the next generation down the river.' This sort of thing was often accompanied by a calculated display of masculine passion. Enormous men with thick moustaches and tattered donkey jackets would glance soulfully towards the ground, bite their tremulous lips and convey a moving (or embarrassing) impression of intolerable suffering. The implication was clear. Democracy is not a matter of counting heads. Democracy means *listening to those who feel most deeply.*

Another source of anxiety in those early days of March was the behaviour of Arthur Scargill, the NUM's worryingly indomitable President. The party line on Scargill had been thoroughly rehearsed by everyone on the left. In public we hailed him as the most principled trade-union leader of the modern age, an outstanding orator and Marxist militant whose ability to unite the rank and file was well-nigh peerless. I myself assured a conservative friend in the first week of the strike that Scargill was a 'great man'. In private a lot of people were rather less effusive. The complaint one heard most often, especially from older activists who knew from bitter experience that dying in the last ditch rarely brings advantages, was that Scargill had a dangerous aversion to compromise. 'Arthur never dilutes his whisky', as a local communist once told me. 'Once he's got his list of demands he sticks to them through thick and thin. It's never occurred to him that achieving some goals occasionally means abandoning others.' These remarks would prove prescient.

My own concern about Scargill was slightly different, and probably stemmed from my chronic habit of perceiving public figures through the prism of my own character flaws. I always felt that there was more than a hint of the nervous only child about him. The idea that he enjoyed a natural bond with the rank and file seemed dubious in the extreme. One only had to look at his chilly blue eyes and his small, twitchingly defensive mouth to see that here was man to whom suspicion came naturally. His ability to unite the miners around his leadership was undoubtedly formidable, but it was never based on gregariousness or good cheer. Scargill's instinct was always to achieve unity through nastiness. Speaking to groups of miners whose enthusiasm could never be guaranteed in advance, he relied more than anything else on scapegoating of the most blatant kind. His speciality was the vindictive anecdote about a hapless member of the 'boss class', delivered in the certain knowledge that nothing brings men together quite as effectively as hatred. His venomous impersonations of rich conservatives, Belgian judges and elderly members of the House of Lords were the stuff of comic legend. As the gales of boisterous laughter rose around him, every last trace of nervousness seemed to drain from his face. Once again his brave, loyal miners had proved that they were worthy of him. Once again he held them in the palms of his hands.

One example. In an interview he gave to *New Left Review* in 1975, Scargill spoke in enthralling detail about his role in the miners' strike of 1972. Much of what he said focused on the so-called 'Battle of Saltley Gate', when mass pickets brought the strike to a successful conclusion by shutting down a coke depot in the Saltley area of Birmingham. Recalling the moment at which the depot was finally closed, Scargill made great play of this semi-farcical exchange with the Chief Constable of the local police:

> The Chief Constable said: 'That's it, I'm not risking any more here, those gates stay closed.' He then turned to me – this is absolutely factual – and said: 'Will you please do us a favour? Will you please disperse the crowd?' And I said on two conditions: firstly that I can make a speech to the crowd. He said, 'Agreed.' And secondly that I can use your equipment, because mine's knackered. He said: 'Agreed.' Then I spoke from the urinal in Birmingham, with this police equipment.

> I gave a political speech to that mass of people and told them that it was the greatest victory of the working class, certainly in my lifetime. The lads who were there were overcome with emotion ...[30]

Here we have the Scargill anecdote in its purest form. The language is colourful, the detail well chosen and the humour extremely malicious. What it offers to its listeners is an alliance based on exclusion. 'Take heart, comrades', one can hear Scargill saying, 'You and I could never be as stupid as that poor bloody policeman! Let us bask in a sense of our shared superiority!' I'm not suggesting that the miners lost the strike because of one man's rhetoric, but neither should the trouble it caused be underestimated. When unity is rooted in cruelty, it begins to decompose as soon as it forms. To laugh at the satirical thrust is to pose the uneasy question 'When will it be turned on me?' Scargill's tragedy was that he destroyed with one hand what he built with the other. Having roused the miners into a paroxysm of collective determination, he had no means of sustaining the mood once the speech was over. The path from 'we are' to 'I am' was shorter than he ever realised.

All our doubts were suppressed. The claim that the strike 'polarised' Britain is about as true as a cliché can be. I assume that Swansea's experience of events was pretty typical. Everywhere you looked there were true believers – those who said that Britain would haemorrhage its decency if the miners lost, and those who said that it would collapse into chaos if they won. People somehow knew that the result of the strike would define the national culture for a generation (as indeed it has) and most of us felt that uncritical support for our own side was a precondition of victory. The only person who went out of his way to dump on the miners was the leader of the Labour Party, who famously associated political respectability with betraying

30 Arthur Scargill, 'The New Unionism', *New Left Review*, No. 92, July-August 1975, p. 19.

his own people.[31]

The NUM won our support with a ruthless appeal to sentimentality. Its spokesmen made a fetish of the word 'community'. We were continually told that the strike's ultimate purpose was to defend a way of life. Thatcher's Britain was groaning under the weight of its own selfishness, or so it was said. It was only in the pit villages of Yorkshire, Scotland or South Wales that the warm glow of solidarity could still be felt. Those windswept industrial redoubts with their overcast skies, gloomy chapels and towering pithead wheels were our last defence against the horrors of the atomised society. Abandon them to their fate and the last traces of human intimacy would disappear with them. I can see now that the NUM's rhetoric of community was a bit like a political Rorschach test. Our responses to it told us more about ourselves than it did about the miners. The people who wept and wailed most noisily about the miners were precisely those whose loneliness was most marked. To bang on about community was effectively to admit that there was something missing in one's own life. Even the unlikeliest specimens of bourgeois refinement were susceptible to it. I can still vividly remember Tony Benn, that most patrician of British socialists, lisping his way through a preposterous tribute to the miners on the programme *Question Time*. The gist of his message was that the miners were infinitely superior to the 'city slickers' (or 'shitty schlickersh', as he seemed to pronounce it) because they 'had to rely on their mates' in the places where it was 'really dirty'. As he spoke he thrust out his clenched fists in a frantic imitation of digging for coal. He looked for all the world liked a man on the edge of despair, and it is probably no coincidence that his career was going downhill at the time.[32]

31 Apparently the following joke was a favourite on the the picket lines: Kinnock, Kinnock. Who's there? Ramsay MacDonald.

32 Tony Benn died while I was correcting the proofs of this book. My uncharitable portrait of him here should not be taken to imply a lack of respect. Benn was one of the greats and every British socialist of my generation learned an enormous amount from him. I consider it a privilege to have met him and to have heard him speak.

Not that I can talk. I peddled the rhetoric of community as enthusiastically as anyone. Nothing gave me greater pleasure than accusing my Scargill-hating friends (to whom I'll return in a moment) of being too emotionally deracinated to appreciate the need for 'solidarity'. Yet my support for the miners was ultimately based on a more fundamental – and perhaps more selfish – impulse which at first I could barely articulate. I only fully came to understand it when I turned up at the reading room of Swansea Library, the site of my first encounter with Marxism, to glance through the day's papers on a chilly afternoon in late November. It must have been about five o'clock and the sky was already dark. Everything conspired to produce an air of resonant loneliness. There was very little traffic on the road outside but from time to time a disembodied voice blew in on the breeze. One envisaged shop workers making their way home with overcoats buttoned to the top and scarves wrapped around their mouths, anxious for a cup of tea and the analgesic of evening television. It was the sort of atmosphere in which epiphanies proliferate.

The agent of revelation was a black-and-white photograph on an inside page of the *Morning Star*. Illustrating an article on how the mining communities were coping with hardship, it depicted a small group of strikers scavenging for shards of coal on the side of a slag heap. The image of a man in the foreground of the photo affected me as deeply as some people are affected by Goya. He was probably a few years shy of fifty and by no means archaic in his appearance, though to my adolescent eyes he looked more like a visitation from the General Strike than a member of the Scargill *fronde*. Wearing a flat cap and a battered woollen jacket, he stood in profile with his hands in his pockets and gazed at the earth in front of him. The look on his face was one of unillusioned expectation. He knew that little enough coal would be found but he was determined to exhaust what was there. The strong wind freezing his earlobes, the taste of coal dust on his tongue and the pain in his thighs as he climbed higher and higher were trivial inconveniences. Here was a man who would not give up until his barren surroundings had yielded their treasure.

All of a sudden I knew how I *really* felt about the Miners' Strike. In a moment of unusual clarity I surmised that the struggle was about a lot more than energy policy, communities or trade unionism. Its real subject was nothing less than the future of industrial civilisation. As a child of the 1970s I had never doubted that advanced technology was the *sine qua non* of civilised life. Endless footage of spaceships, skyscrapers and robots had taught me that the capacity to remake the environment in our own image was humanity's cardinal virtue. Yet I also knew (or thought I knew) that the gains of science were under threat from affluence. People of my generation were simply too pampered, too enfeebled by consumerism's fluffy embrace to throw everything into the battle against nature. Who among us would be as self-sacrificing as a Louis Pasteur or a Rosalind Franklin, stoically poisoning their own bodies in pursuit of ever greater knowledge? That's why the miners mattered so much. Every time they sank into the earth and wrestled tons of coal from narrow seams, every time they risked their lives in subterranean passages held up by groaning props, they symbolised the Promethean impulse in all its bloody-minded heroism. Either we would tame nature or nature would tame us – that seemed to be their philosophy. If men like the ones in the photograph were defeated, Britain would lose its shock troops in the war against the elements.

My other reason for suppressing my doubts about the miners was that my friends were such a pain in the arse. For a couple of years before I went to university in 1985 I mixed primarily with the children of the Swansea *petty bourgeoisie*. God knows how I fell in with them. Most of them were sixth-formers at an undistinguished but violently snobbish private (not public!) school which operated out of a converted townhouse in St. James's Crescent. I suppose I liked them because they represented the path not taken. Like me they were second-generation middle class, but unlike me (the only one among them who wore a donkey jacket with a CND badge on the lapel) they tried to deal with their social anxieties by embracing Thatcherite chauvinism in its most naked form. Secretly ashamed of their plebeian grandparents, desperate to disguise the last traces of *arriviste* vulgarity in their accents, they took enormous pleasure in embracing every saloon-bar prejudice in the book. The trade unions had destroyed the country and had to be banned. Poverty was largely self-inflicted. The blacks were all right in their way but there were too many of them in the country. Nelson Mandela was nothing but a terrorist.

Right from the start of the Strike I debated the issues with them every week. On Fridays and Saturdays we usually went drinking at an upmarket hotel that overlooked the beach. Defiantly ill-dressed in an oasis of gleaming mirrors, plush chairs and mock-Tudor beams, I patiently explained to them that it was in their own best interests if the NUM won: 'No one in this room is so well off that he can afford to see the trade unions destroyed!' Then they queued up to impale my head on a stick and parade it around the bar, singing the praises of Mrs Thatcher, Ian MacGregor and the British police force as they went. Certain phrases and injunctions tended to reoccur like pogroms in a civil war: 'Commie idiot!', 'I tell you the miners are just *trash*!', 'Go back to Russia!' It got to the point where I responded to each new event in the strike by wondering how my friends would use it to torture me. When two Welsh miners threw a breezeblock off a motorway bridge and killed a taxi driver who was ferrying a strikebreaker to work, I caught myself thinking 'Oh shit – what am I going to say in the pub on Saturday?'

Every week I squirmed with embarrassment as Swansea's aspiring poujadistes lambasted me for my naiveté, and every week my support for the miners grew. Things hit a memorable low in the first few days of December. The journal *Marxism Today*, organ of what some people wrongly called the 'eurocommunist' wing of the Communist Party, had launched an appeal to raise money for the miners and their families at Christmas. Buoyed up by a generous response from my relatives, I unwisely supposed that I could talk my friends into contributing on purely humanitarian grounds. No such luck. My first port of call was a slovenly little bigot called Peredur, notorious for his abuse of the double negative, who later became a second-hand car salesman and one of Swansea's most porcine men. As he leaned against the bar with his head framed by a neon sign reading 'Happy Christmas', he told me that he'd prefer to eat his own turds than contribute to a strike fund. 'But surely you'd like to see the children in the mining communities have a good Christmas?', I asked him. 'Not if they're miners' children', he replied.

I cannot think of another moment at which my commitment to the cause burned more ferociously. There is much to be said for the self-righteousness of youth.

I suspect that most strikes are only truly eventful for the people who are directly caught up in them. A picket, a policeman or a politician can look forward to a lengthy period of high drama once the factory gates have shut. For the multitude of people on the margins of the strike – the local traders, the relatives of the strikers, the political activists with their newspapers and collecting tins – things usually pass off more quietly. My own experience of the Miners' Strike was embarrassingly becalmed. Although I collected money, distributed literature and attended meetings, I was never involved in the sort of era-defining activities that are still remembered more than twenty years later. Not for me the snarling confrontation with the tooled-up policeman or the heroic attempt to shield violent pickets from what we used to call 'class justice'. I suppose I was simply too young, too lackadaisical and too cowardly to work for the miners as tirelessly as I should have. Having said all that, a couple of eerily emblematic events have stuck in my mind. Neither was very dramatic or significant by the standards of the people at the heart of the strike, but both of them unsettled me at the time and unsettle me now. They occurred within a week of each other in early December, exactly at the point when the

NUM's more thoughtful supporters were beginning to worry that victory might not be ours.

The first of these events took place on a bitterly cold Saturday in Swansea. The South Wales region of the NUM was due to hold a march through the city in the early afternoon, followed by a rally at the leisure centre. For a few delirious hours the left took charge of the streets. I had just been rereading *Homage to Catalonia*, swept away for the umpteenth time by its description of revolutionary Barcelona in 1936, and looking around me I fancied I knew what Orwell meant when he said 'It was the first time that I had ever been in a town where the working class was in the saddle.'[33] Even before the march began the place was humming with plebeian intensity. The pavements were thronged with miners, steelworkers and other swarthy behemoths from our industrial hinterland. Most of them had resolved to ignore (or defy) the weather and went ostentatiously coatless, their flimsy jumpers covered with stickers bearing the slogans of the moment: 'Coal not Dole', 'Victory to the Miners', 'Kick Out the Tories'. As they strutted noisily along, never pushing anyone into the road but taking it as their due when the crowds parted in front of them, they gave the impression that solidarity – the sheer irrepressible pleasure of saying 'All for one and one for all' – had imbued their limbs with a sort of pneumatic strength. Pavements weren't so much pounded as pulverised. As I drank in the scene I wouldn't have been surprised if a slag heap had appeared above High Street, tubs of coal had flowed down Constitution Hill or someone had started a greyhound race outside Marks and Spencer. It seemed as if the culture of the valleys had overlaid itself on Swansea's sleepy streets and manhandled us into new life. If I ever doubted that 'civilisation ... is built on coal' (another Orwellian *bon mot*),[34] I doubted it no longer.

Making my way past one of the rowdier pubs near the

33 George Orwell, *Homage to Catalonia* (London: Penguin, 2000 [1938]), p. 2.

34 George Orwell, *The Road to Wigan Pier* (London: Penguin, 2001 [1937]), p. 18.

shopping centre, I thought I heard someone shouting my name above the din. Out of the corner of my eye I glimpsed a thick-set ruffian in a donkey jacket exploding out of the doorway and charging towards me. The next thing I knew he was rubbing my face in his chest and ruffling my hair with beery vigour. 'All right, comrade?', he boomed, 'Are you still a virgin?' It was Julian. I hadn't seen or heard from him since he caught an early train to London over a year earlier, heading – or so he claimed – for an apprenticeship at an anarchist printshop in the East End. The transformation was incredible. Back in our Crass days he had a mane of black hair, a mild problem with puppy fat and a Gothically pale complexion. Now his head was completely shaved, his muscles were rippling and his face was as ruddy as a Lancashire farmer's. The donkey jacket was set off by some brutally faded jeans and a pair of cherry-red boots. The badge on his lapel said 'They Shall Not Pass!'

I resented him enormously for pushing off to London and forgetting all about me, but I could hardly pretend that I wasn't delighted to see him. His importance in my life was too great for that. In one way or another I associated him with all the most seminal moments of my adolescence, from the Crass gig on the Sandfields Estate to the discovery of Orwell and the revelatory encounter with the Socialist Party of Great Britain. Our friendship was effectively over but in the back of my mind I still thought of him as a co-conspirator. As he took me by the elbow and pushed me into the pub, I sensed that the old connection had been re-established in an instant.

The atmosphere inside was pleasingly proletarian. A curtain of smoke hung in the air like fog and thunderous heavy metal seared out from the jukebox. Julian introduced me with a dismissive 'This is Phil' to a group of about fifteen friends, most of whom looked exactly like him – hard, edgy, political. Then he shouted something into the ear of a painfully sexy girl in a black leather jacket and a tartan mini-skirt, pushed his way to the bar and came back with two glasses of vodka and orange. I was pleased to see that he remembered my tipple. We sat on a pair of stools near the door and he told me about his time in London. It turned out that he'd abandoned anarchism more or less as soon as he arrived, exasperated beyond endurance by the 'witless meanderings of bearded wankers'. Lowering his voice as if the information he was about to convey was enough to get him arrested, he said that he'd drifted around the left for a while and eventually become a member of the 'Squaddists'. He started to explain but I knew exactly what he meant. The Squaddists were a small but ultra-committed group of Trotskyists, mostly ex-members of the Socialist Workers Party, who had made a name for themselves by conducting a violent campaign against fascism.[35] Armed with bricks, bottles and baseball bats (and sometimes with even deadlier weaponry – pickaxes were widely favoured), they had set themselves the goal of ridding the public square of every last semblance of far-right activity. This had involved breaking up meetings of the National Front and the British National Party, brawling with newspaper sellers from the British Movement and invading the homes of any fascist whose address had been made public. Blood had flowed in copious quantities and Julian had inflicted his fair share of wounds. His friends at the bar were fellow Squaddists, some from Cardiff but most from London, who had travelled down to Swansea to protect the march against a rumoured attack from the British Movement.

I should have been appalled. Prematurely middle-aged in my commitment to what some on the left called 'parliamentary cretinism', I had always believed that arguing with fascists was much to be preferred to beating them to a pulp. But this was not a day for constitutional proprieties. The excitement that coursed through my system as Julian spoke could hardly be gainsaid. At the height of our friendship we had often joked about 'peak-experience moments' – moments when the combined effect of teenage enthusiasm, naive self-regard and boyish comradeship

35 For a vivid and slightly disturbing account of the Squaddists and other organisations associated with militant anti-fascism, see Dave Hann and Steve Tilzey, *No Retreat: The Secret War Between Britain's Anti-Fascists and the Far Right* (Lytham: Milo Book, 2003).

was a surging, exhilarating, irrepressible sense that anything was possible. Here was a peak experience of unparalleled intensity. The blood gushed noisily through my ears, the adrenaline flowed torrentially through my stomach as I thought about Julian and his comrades dishing out rough justice to fascists on the street. It was absurd to suppose that someone as scrawny as me could ever make the grade as an urban warrior, yet the knowledge that I'd never be a Squaddist didn't seem to matter. For the first time in my life I knew why so many people regarded political violence as the most romantic thing in the world.

Julian's startling political narrative wasn't the only thing fuelling my mood. The vodka had undoubtedly played its part, titillating my pleasure centres with its blowsy caresses. There was also the extraordinary fact that the girl in the leather jacket and the mini skirt appeared to be flirting with me. She had come over about ten minutes into the conversation, leaned on the table and draped her right arm over my shoulders. Apparently her name was Helen. Everytime I said anything she dilated her irises and smiled encouragingly. For a quarter of an hour or so I dared to think that she'd taken a fancy to me, but then – seeing her wink at Julian and seeing him grin back mischievously – I realised what was going on. It was all a set-up. Still exasperated by my serial failures with women (and realising at a glance that my luck hadn't changed during his absence), Julian had immediately resumed his role as my sexual *doktorvater* and instructed Helen to be nice to me. So now I knew what he'd said to her at the bar! I couldn't decide whether to feel outraged or amused. In the end, on the well-known principle that critics of the free market can't be choosers, I decided to ride my luck as far as it would go.

The threatened attack by the British Movement failed to materialise, which was probably just as well. None of the Squaddists was sober enough to defend the march against anything. My own progress through the streets of Swansea was undignified in the extreme. Flanked by Julian on my left and Helen on my right, I spent most of the march giggling like a hardened alcoholic. The banners, the placards and the sound of the NUM band would normally have moved me deeply. Now I just found them funny. My refusal to take anything seriously persisted into the rally, where I spent more time admiring Helen's arse than listening to the speeches. My sexual reverie only came to an end when the Squaddists showed their dark side. The cause of the trouble was a thin, slightly nerdish young man who started heckling during the final speech. As far as I could tell he was shouting things like 'Why no ballot?' and 'Make Scargill accountable to his members!' in an accent at once posh, lispy and ineffectual.[36] When it became clear that he intended to heckle indefinitely, one of Julian's Squaddist friends sidled up to him and told him to cut it out. The instruction was ignored. Then a group of five or six Squaddists went over and formed an arc around him, hoping to intimidate him into silence with some menacing body language. This too was unsuccessful. The rally was reaching its climax. A lack of unanimity could not be allowed. Locking his arm behind his back and propelling him forward with a knee to the upper thigh, one of the Squaddists bundled the heckler out of the door and threw him down on the grass outside. About sixty people followed with the scent of blood in their nostrils.

I was deeply shocked by this turn of events, perhaps because the weedy young man with the democratic scruples reminded me so much of myself. Shock turned to useless indignation as the Squaddists began to humiliate him for their own pleasure. They didn't beat him up but three of them straddled his prostrate body and laughed themselves silly while he struggled to get free. The others gathered around like a pack of Trotskyist jackals, punching the sky with their clenched fists and singing tuneless versions of socialist songs. At this point I was joined by Helen, who was enjoying the spectacle as much as any of them. Her eyes flashing in a pale and rather bovine imitation of seductiveness, she put her arms around me and started stroking

36 I later discovered that he was a novitiate member of the Revolutionary Communist Party, whose belief that the NUM leadership was behaving too autocratically had made it very unpopular in the mining communities.

my buttocks. I suddenly realised that I was being offered a deal. If I made it clear that I approved of what was going on, if I stamped and sang and shouted like all the rest of them, I could expect a very pleasurable reward as the day wore on. I will never forget the sensation of something dark, weak and discreditable being unlocked in the depths of my being. It was perhaps the only time in my life when I felt truly disinhibited. Flinging my arms around Helen and turning my delighted gaze on the still-imprisoned heckler, I allowed a torrent of sadistic laughter to unleash itself in my throat. The hour of rough proletarian justice was upon us. My tonsils rasped like sandpaper as I joined the others in a chaotic rendition of 'The Internationale': 'Arise ye starvelings from your slumbers/Arise ye criminals of want'. Helen gave me a kiss on the cheek to ensure that I didn't lose momentum. So this was what solidarity was all about.

Three or four days after my initiation at the rally, still suffering slightly from the combined effects of adrenaline, vodka and lust, I had to attend a funeral. Over the previous twelve months a good friend of the family had slowly been dying of cancer. The course of her illness had done a great deal to strip away the more consoling assumptions of my childhood. Like most people born in comfortable circumstances I had always cleaved to a sort of unreflective dualism. It seemed to me that the spirit could be trained to resist the weaknesses of the body, even to the point where the seriously ill or the very old could steel themselves to ignore the imminence of their own deaths. None of these assumptions survived the experience of watching Anna die. A teacher in her early sixties, popular among several generations of pupils, she had once been widely admired for her streak of buxom irreverence. Now her personality seemed to fade away in exact proportion to the hollowing out of her cheeks. The spirit trailed the flesh in a relationship of strict necessity.

It was the first time I'd ever been to a funeral, and the first time I'd been in a church since I'd given a reading at a Christmas service when I was ten. The weather did what it always does at burials in South Wales and provided a dispiriting backdrop for our gloomiest thoughts. There was a persistent drizzle all morning, the temperature was Arctic and the glowering sky leeched the colour out of the stained glass windows. As I glanced at the gleaming mahogany panel at the foot of Anna's coffin, I couldn't resist the thought that it was probably more cheerful inside the box than outside it. Then I apologised to the Hidden God for my stupid impiety.

The minister who took the service had been a friend of Anna's and spoke about her warmly. Tall, distinguished and eloquent with a shock of grey hair falling onto his forehead, he conjured a vivid picture of a rambunctious personality. 'I will always remember her', he said, 'stalking through the Uplands with a copy of *The Times* under her arm and a look of quiet determination on her quizzical face.' Perhaps he overdid it a bit. The more clearly he brought her to our minds the worse we all felt. Her relatives in the front row seemed frozen in an agony of inwardness, as if the only way they could maintain their composure was to monitor the beating of their own hearts. For a moment I genuinely thought they were paralysed.

Even in the middle of a funeral service I found it difficult to set my political obsessions to one side. The sight of so many suffering people inspired some disconcerting thoughts about the nature of commitment. Whenever I'd visited Anna during her illness, I often found that my interest in socialism deserted me for a few hours. All my cherished ideas about workers' control, industrial growth and direct democracy seemed horribly out of sync with the spectacle of decaying flesh. These feelings of political quietism came flooding back as the service wore on. Everywhere I looked I saw people who had been diminished by Anna's death. The grandchildren in trendy suits, the colleagues in teachers' subfusc and the bridge-playing friends in pleated skirts were gripped by a sense that life could not be trusted. Because I was young and naive and unwilling to admit to my own insensitivity, I was absolutely certain that none of us would ever recover. How absurd to believe that a people so weak, so vulnerable to the infirmities of the flesh could ever be happy or creative or free! Self-dramatising even in my moment of agony, I found myself casting around for an aphorism that would sum everything up, a couple of sentences of sub-Sartrean wisdom that would pronounce the death rites over my years of hope. The best I could manage was this: 'Hope is a liar. It only flourishes when it tells us that the body is our friend.'

The wake was held in a nearby church hall. Afterwards I walked through the churchyard on my own, searingly unhappy but warming to the role of the tragic young man who sees too deeply. It was almost dusk and the weather was no more hospitable than it had been earlier. Anna was being buried in the same grave as her parents and the gravedigger was still at work. When he saw me coming he wiped the soil from his hands, gave me a cheery but commiserative smile ('Don't worry, mate – you'll soon be feeling better!', or so he seemed to say) and asked me whether I wanted him to disappear while I paid my last respects. Not at all, I assured him. There didn't seem much point.

He looked me up and down and winced slightly at my evident lack of robustness. It was clear from the start that he was a bit of a Jack the lad, the sort of affable maverick who sustains a streak of adolescent irreverence well into middle age. Bearded, muscular and strangely serene, he made a few rueful remarks about the ghastliness of the weather and the indignity of the gravedigger's lot. Then he told me that gravedigging wasn't his usual line of work. 'Oh really?', I replied, 'What do you normally do?' 'I'm a miner', he said.

I blush with embarrassment at the thought of how quickly my mood changed. A little flutter of excitement passed across the upper reaches of my stomach, and in a matter of seconds my despair had lifted. Here at last was a bona fide representative of the working class in struggle! I asked him whether he was on strike and he said that he was. Stumbling over my words I told him how fervently I supported the cause, how much I admired the miners' heroism and how enthusiastically I'd collected money, distributed leaflets and attended rallies. For the second time in less than five minutes he cast a sceptical eye across my puny frame, suppressing the urge to burst into laughter at my display of adolescent fervour. 'Tell me', he said, 'do you believe that the miners deserve to have a say in how their own lives are run?' I told him that I did. 'In that case', he asked me, 'why didn't Scargill allow us a vote on whether or not we should strike?'

The question was so unexpected it set my ears ringing. My first flesh-and-blood miner was no hardened militant but a member of the Scargill-hating awkward squad. It turned out that he was one of the majority in South Wales who had initially opted not to strike, in his case because his teenage daughter had leukaemia and he didn't want to condemn her to a comfortless existence. The only thing that kept him away from the pit was the violence of the men on the picket lines, one of whom had told him that his daughter would be 'dying even earlier than scheduled' if he failed to join the struggle. Even then he had not gone down without a fight. In the first few weeks of the strike he acquired a reputation for storming into the local Labour club, striding up to prominent members of the strike committee ('... those fuckers can always afford a pint ...') and accusing them of cowardice. His reward had been a visit in the middle of the night from a deputation of 'Scotch Cattle' – a phrase he used unselfconsciously but which I, to my shame, had never heard before. In a piece of breathless storytelling worthy of Alexander Cordell (in retrospect I'm inclined to think that his anecdotes owed more to *Rape of the Fair Country* than to his own experience), he told me how five or six men in balaclavas had gathered in his backyard and banged iron bars against the fence, the walls and the door. Apparently they stopped short of storming the house but one of them poured lighter fuel into the bin and set fire to its contents, shouting 'You'll be next!' with guttural urgency as the flames whooshed into the sky. After that there were no more shows of defiance. He salved his dignity by refusing any money from the strike fund and doing odd jobs around the valley. The opportunity to dig graves had come through a 'good as gold' brother-in-law who knew a few people on the council. It was his proud boast that he had never stood on the picket line.

Thrown back on my meagre polemical resources, I muttered something about the individual having to suffer in order that the collective could flourish. That really tore it. 'Haven't you understood *anything*?', he asked. 'No one is going to benefit from this strike. No one at all. Individual or collective, Scargillite or blackleg – *everyone's* going to fucking lose!' In the back of my mind I'd always assumed that 'ordinary people' had a shaky grasp on public affairs. What came next cured me of that view forever. Flinging his arms around like a barker at an old-time music hall, grinning openly at my discomfort without ever losing his air of geniality, my didactic gravedigger spat out a masterful account of where the strike had gone wrong. The core of his case was that the NUM was still fighting the industrial battles of the 1970s, not realising that conditions had changed decisively. Margaret Thatcher was no Edward Heath. Her government had been preparing for a scrap for ages and there was nothing it wouldn't stoop to. There was no point using flying pickets when the pit villages were bristling with policemen on horseback. Every court in the land was itching to sequestrate the union's funds: 'Arthur Scargill is a better gravedigger than I am myself. The only problem is that he's buried the miners' hopes.'

The flow was astonishing. Words streamed across the afternoon like Welsh lager being poured from an unusually tall bottle. At one point I contemplated a prolier-than-thou response – something along the lines of 'How dare you insult a heroic group of men who are sacrificing everything to defend their communities?' – but his closing flourish silenced me for good:

> We could have been back in work six months ago. As you know [he strongly implied that I *didn't* know], the government offered to review its closure programme if the NUM called off the strike.[37] Even the Bolshiest miner in my village thought it

37 Matters weren't as simple as this, though at the time I was too ignorant

was a good deal. It gave us the opportunity to dust ourselves down and return to the pits with dignity. If Scargill still had the sense he was born with, he'd have realised that it gave his blessed union the chance to live and fight another day. Instead he blathered on about not compromising and our last chance was lost. And why? *Because he never asked the rest of us what we thought.*

The following day, shaken beyond belief by my confrontation with working-class conservatism, I put some of these points to to a prominent Swansea communist. 'I wouldn't waste your time with arguments like that', he told me. 'Most of them have been cooked up by the *Daily Mail.* No working man would take them seriously.'

Everyone seems to know where they were and what they were doing when they heard that the Miners' Strike had been called off. Personally I have no clear recollection of where I was, which strikes me now as slightly odd. What I remember very vividly is watching the news some hours after the announcement and being deeply shocked by the spectacle of vanquished power. The NUM's executive committee had met that afternoon and unwillingly decided that the miners should go back to work. To his credit, Scargill immediately went outside and addressed a boisterous group of militants who were calling for the strike to be prolonged. It was no longer a case of cometh the hour, cometh the man. Knowing that his reception was likely to be a rocky one ('rocky' being a Labour Movement euphemism for coruscatingly awful), Scargill resorted with uncommendable speed to the most touchy-feely language he could muster. Pale and clearly devastated, he thanked the militants 'from the bottom of my heart' for their loyalty during the strike. He really needn't have bothered. Jabbing the air with their forefingers

to realise it. For a clear account of the deal that the NUM was offered in July 1984, see Paul Routledge, *Scargill: The Unauthorized Biography* (London: Harper Collins, 1993), p. 158f.

like a terraceful of angry football fans, his erstwhile supporters drowned him out with a magnificently defiant chant of 'We're not going back! We're not going back!' Scargill bit his lip, spun a little unsteadily on his heels and returned to the sanctuary of the NUM's headquarters. The carnival of the oppressed was over.

In the end I became a Scargill heckler myself. Let me tell you about it. Scargill has made a number of appearances in Swansea since the end of the strike. Over the last ten years he has usually been speaking in support of the Socialist Labour Party (SLP), the organisation he founded after leaving the Labour Party in 1996. The last time he was here was the day before the Welsh elections in 2007, when he addressed an SLP rally in the Unitarian church on High Street. I went along in a spirit of residual piety, accompanied by my partner Jasmine. Never let it be said that I fail to take my loved ones to the most glamorous events.

It was all rather pitiful. Only about fifteen people turned up and several of them had been shipped in from the valleys. In an unconscious expression of contempt for his audience, Scargill had abandoned his customary shirt-and-tie and wore an open-necked check shirt, navy trousers and a pair of austere black shoes. At the age of sixty-nine he still gave off a powerful air of tensed muscularity, and not even his bald head (the site of some much-satirised 'combovers' during the glory days of the strike) could reduce the impression of columnar defiance. The oratory was another matter. There was to be no repetition of the audacious flow, soaring emotionalism and vicious wit of yesteryear. The sad truth is that Scargill came across as a man in almost pathological need of praise. Gazing out at his acolytes, all of them well-meaning sentimentalists who couldn't accept that the pits had long since been shut, he spoke for nearly an hour in sustained tribute to himself. King Arthur had arrived at his threadbare Camelot and demanded due deference.

Scargill has never understood the distinction between showing and telling. Instead of describing his role in the events of the past and leaving us to draw the appropriate conclusions, he used a sort of oratorical spray can to underscore his eminence.

At one point he actually told us that 'My very close friend Tony Benn has said that I'm the greatest trade-union leader in British history.' (The shade of Arthur Horner was heard to mutter 'Steady on, boyo' somewhere near the rafters.) His other tactic was to rub our noses in our own ignorance, in the expectation that we would look to his capacious and prophetic brain to provide us with the knowledge we lacked. Ten times or more he began a point by saying 'I bet you don't know that ... ' or 'You're probably not aware that ... ' or 'Let me tell you something that perhaps you don't know'. As I listened I felt a familiar swelling in the gut that could only mean one thing: I was going to cause trouble in the question-and-answer sesssion.

And so I did. Since the entire evening had been given over to leader worship, I decided to ask Scargill about his attitude to democracy. Revolving a pen in my hands in what I hoped was a display of unflappable sangfroid, I made a characteristically wordy intervention:

'Mr Scargill spoke very powerfully about the erosion of democracy in modern Britain. This might have led us to suppose that the internal affairs of his own party are always conducted on scrupulously democratic lines. Unfortunately that isn't always the case. Mr Scargill and his allies in the leadership of the SLP have resorted to some strikingly autocratic methods over the last ten years. Chief among them was the introduction in 1997 of a block vote, wielded in the name of the 3000 members of a retired miners' association, which Mr Scargill has used to outvote the SLP's rank and file at party conferences. My question to Mr Scargill is this: How is his autocratic leadership of the SLP consistent with his undoubted belief in extending democracy in the wider society?'

My initial compliment had prompted a nod of the head from Scargill, who took it for granted that a further display of deference was underway. By the time I'd finished he clearly saw me as an insolent cockroach who needed trampling underfoot. There was no question of an eirenic or a more-in-sorrow-than-in-anger sort of reply. Nothing but utter humiliation would do.

Fixing me with a look of sneering contempt – the sort of look he must have used fifty years earlier when offering a troublesome classmate outside – he told me that the block vote to which I referred had existed since before 1997: 'If you're going to ask a question, you have to get your facts right.' At this point I had a clear but unappetising choice. Either I could remain silent and allow the Scargill tank to leave its treadmarks all over my corduroy jacket, or else I could answer back and hope that my voice didn't tremble too much. In the event I did the unthinkable and heckled one of the twentieth-century's greatest orators:

'Mr Scargill', I said as firmly as I could, 'the block vote was used for the first time at your Conference in 1997.'

At the risk of sounding my own foghorn, I think it's fair to say that my little act of hubris had a pleasingly deflationary effect. Scargill winced for a second or two, exhaled in exasperation and seemed to lose a couple of inches as his shoulders sank towards his midriff. His only response was to repeat his assertion that I'd got my facts wrong. Sensing that he'd been caught momentarily off balance, I decided to increase the insolence quotient by doing some repetition of my own:

'Mr Scargill [this time I intoned the words with a certain schoolmasterly iciness], the block vote was deployed for the first time at the SLP's conference in 1997.'

Astonishingly enough, the best he could do was to accuse me of factual inaccuracy for a third time. This allowed me to land a blow that certainly hurt him more than it hurt me: 'Neither of us is in a position to prove that what he says is true, so please get on with answering the question. Surely that's not asking too much?'

The exchanges went on for another five minutes and involved a lot of petulance on both sides. I couldn't say I'd won but neither could I say I'd lost. As the Chairwoman thanked Scargill for coming and we gave him an appreciative round of applause, Jasmine shot me an impish grin which suggested that I hadn't done too badly. I was pleased to hold the mighty Scargill to a not-very-honourable draw.

Then something rather absurd happened. Before Jasmine and I had a chance to leave our seats, Scargill was hurrying towards us and saying 'Hang on, comrades, I want to explain my position on the block vote.' He sat down about a foot away and nodded affably when I gave him a copy of an anti-fascist newspaper which I'd been hawking around. I listened politely as he made a frankly unconvincing case about the democratic rationale for block votes. His determination to win my support was rather touching. No longer overawed, I launched into a patronising lecture on the internal history of the Labour Party. I made all the obvious points: The block vote had been introduced into the Party by the right wing. Its purpose had always been to allow the leadership to outvote the rank and file. Throughout the Fifties, Sixties and Seventies – the years of the Bevanite and Bennite insurgencies – it had enabled the likes of Gaitskell, Wilson and Callaghan to mount a holding operation against genuine socialist policies. When Scargill tried to interrupt me I heard myself say 'Hang on a minute, Mr Scargill – I've listened to your opinion and I respect it. But please let me finish.'

The conversation only came to an end when a man known as 'Irish Mick', a ridiculous old sycophant who'd been calling out 'hear, hear' all evening, came over to slap his leader on the back and swap stories about picket lines, police brutality and the victories of the past. Realising that the block vote would have to wait for another day, Scargill seemed happy enough to shake my hand and abandon me to the revisionist night. Just think about it. Here was a man who once had the power to bring down governments. Now he was reduced to debating with me in a drafty church in a provincial city. How's that for a case of The Forward March of Labour Halted?

CHAPTER 5
An Invitation to the Party

The Miners' Strike was a time of major defeats and small but significant victories. At the very moment when the Labour Movement sank to the floor in agony, opportunities for new beginnings seemed to spring up everywhere. It turned out that the miners' message of hope was so powerful, so redolent with the sense that anything was possible, that it lingered in people's minds even when the strike began to crumble. Realising that the path of collective advance was about to be blocked off, thousands of us suddenly dared to believe that our vague dreams of self-improvement could be realised. Factory workers took out bank loans and bought chip shops, pubs or window-cleaning businesses, swapping boredom on the production line for the stimulations of commerce. Housewives demanded a bit more from life than the kitchen sink. Flamboyant teenagers began to think that a place in drama school might not be so unrealistic after all. As for me, I joined the Communist Party and read a lot of books.

The Party in Swansea had never been easy to track down. Unlike the Trotskyist groups it didn't have members selling literature on the streets, nor did it have much of a presence (at least to the uninitiated eye) at demonstrations, marches and public meetings. Yet in one way or another it had a curious ability to draw people into its orbit. I first came across it in the summer of 1982 when the National Eisteddfod was held in Singleton Park near the Uplands. Most of the left groups had hired tents for the week and did their best to peddle newspapers, posters and badges to credulous misfits like me. The communist tent was darker than all the others, less well-stocked with fripperies and manned by a truly terrifying woman whose influence on my life persists to this day. As she looked at me suspiciously through a pair of NHS spectacles with absurdly thick lenses, I reached into the pocket of my jeans and fished out 40p for a copy of the party programme. Its title was *The British Road to Socialism*. Once I became a member of the cognoscenti I would refer to it knowingly as the BRS.

No political manifesto has ever emitted a more powerful sense of urgency. Its front cover depicted a red flag fluttering against a backdrop of uncompromising black. Its chapter headings were at once boldly declamatory and thrillingly laconic: 'Why Britain Needs Socialism', 'The Forces For Change In Britain', 'Towards Socialist Revolution', 'Building A Socialist Britain'. As soon as I left the tent I hurried off to a café just outside the park, ordered a cup of tea and began to read. Almost immediately I found myself veering between emotional extremes. The opening section of the BRS provoked attraction and repulsion in equal measure. What I liked about it was its stately air of democratic respectability. It said quite clearly that socialism could be achieved through parliament and that a socialist Britain would have free elections, a multitude of competing parties (including those which favoured capitalism) and the rule of law. What I disliked about it was the following sentence, whose grimly lowering effect I can still recall nearly thirty years later: 'In 1917 the Russian Revolution led the way, and the world's first socialist system was established in the USSR.'[38] Still in thrall to the SPGB and tolerably well-versed in the rudiments of Trotskyism, I recoiled from the idea that the Kremlin's dark empire could ever be seen as socialist. Was the British road perhaps more potholed than I wanted to admit?

I wrestled with the dilemma for nearly two years. Whenever I felt tempted to get in touch with the Party, inspired by its vision of a scrupulously democratic and serenely constitutional path

38 Communist Party of Great Britain, *The British Road to Socialism*, fifth edition (London: The Communist Party, 1978), p. 11.

to socialism, I remembered its support for the Soviet Union and had second thoughts. In the end it was History with a capital 'H' that forced me to overcome my scruples. As the Miners' Strike got underway and desperate pickets confronted surly policemen less than twenty miles from my home, I realised with a sudden jolt of conscience that my non-joining individualism was no longer enough. Signing up to one of the organisations that supported the NUM was the least I could do. My decision to join the Communist Party (as opposed to the Labour Party or one of the proliferating Trotskyist outfits) was the consequence of a minor epiphany in a Swansea bookshop. On a cold Wednesday morning, browsing aimlessly through the History section of T John Penry on St. Helen's Road, I came across a copy of Hywel Francis's magnificent *Miners Against Fascism: Wales and the Spanish Civil War* (1984). By a strange twist of fate the book fell open at a strikingly evocative photograph from 1926.[39] Taken by a deeply inexpert photographer at the Miners' Institute in Mardy, it depicted a handful of local communists posing stiffly against an expansive banner and a quirky portrait.[40] The banner, complete with an ornate hammer and sickle and the standard quotation from the *Communist Manifesto* ('Proletarians of all Countries, Unite!'), had been sent to the Welsh miners by their Soviet counterparts during the General Strike. The portrait was an extremely crude likeness of Lenin addressing a meeting. Scanning the curiously reserved faces of those long-forgotten activists, I was struck by the quiet sincerity of their belief in the socialist future. For two or three seconds the barriers between the past and the present broke down. In a moment of total

39 See Hywel Francis, *Miners Against Fascism: Wales and the Spanish Civil War* (London: Lawrence and Wishart, 1984). The photograph which made such an impression on me is the second of eight illustrations sandwiched between pages 94 and 95.

40 In the years between the wars, Mardy was one of a handful of mining villages in Britain that were known colloquially as 'Little Moscows' because of their strong communist leanings. See Stuart Macintyre, *Little Moscows: Communism and Working-Class Militancy in Inter-War Britain* (London: Croom Helm, 1980).

conviction I realised that everything I had read was true: *No one had fought for the Welsh miners with as much passion and courage as the communists.* After that my fate was sealed. I attended my first Party meeting the following week.

My *entrée* to the Swansea Branch was effected by the same person who'd sold me a copy of *The British Road to Socialism.* By coincidence I saw her on the street a couple of days after I'd taken the decision to join. She still looked pretty forbidding but I summoned up the courage to approach her and inquire about the whereabouts of the next Branch meeting. It turned out that her name was Linda and she said she'd be delighted to introduce me to the 'other comrades' if I turned up at Dynevor School on Thursday evening. So that's what I did. The meeting was held in a rundown classroom on the second floor. Someone had added a dash of colour to the proceedings by taping a 'Coal not Dole' poster to the blackboard. From time to time the sound of a police siren swept in from the city centre.

Most of the twenty or so people in the room were older than me by forty or fifty years. The dominant mood was one of radical earnestness balanced by avuncular generosity. Those highly articulate men in their respectable jackets and sturdy shoes passionately wanted the miners to win (and more than that: they made no secret of their desire to see the NUM bring down the government), but their attitude towards the process of debate was almost comically scrupulous. What mattered to them above all else was that no one should be left out. The chairman was a genial pensioner called Bob whose phenomenal evenhandedness seems staggering in retrospect. Aware that the Branch was factionalised in at least three directions, he took care to ensure that representatives of each group had a chance to say their piece. Every speaker was allotted the same amount of time as all the others. Any hint of sarcasm or disrespect was stymied by a playful tap on the desk. When the discussion came to an end, Bob summed up the various positions with a sort of saintly disinterestedness. In all the years since I've never met anyone who took such obvious pride in refusing to misrepresent his opponents' opinions.

That first meeting in Dynevor might not have affected me as deeply as my first encounter with the SPGB, but it went a long way towards resolving my doubts about joining the Party. I can even remember the precise moment at which I realised I'd made the right choice. Shortly before the end of the meeting, emboldened by the sense that anything I said would be listened to respectfully, I made a rather faltering point about the unwisdom of drawing too much attention to Soviet support for the NUM. Before anyone could intervene to expose my windy platitudes for what they were, Bob congratulated me warmly on my eloquence and encouraged the rest of the Branch to learn from what I was saying: 'Out of the mouths of babes, comrades – out of the mouths of babes!' The extraordinary thing was that he seemed to be sincere. After forty years in the Party – forty years of witheringly intense debates and innumerable setbacks – he took it entirely for granted that a boy of sixteen had something to teach him. I knew perfectly well that I would not encounter this attitude in any other party. As I returned Bob's encouraging smile and self-consciously brushed some dust from my sleeve, I came to a conclusion that even now I would hesitate to gainsay: In spite of what everyone said, Britain's communists were democratic to the ends of their chewed fingernails.

My faith in the Party's democratic credentials only increased as the weeks wore on. Although they were much too elderly to think of me as their friend, my new comrades tried to make me feel at home by telling me about their lives. It was immediately clear that they formed a distinct fraction of a remarkable generation. Most of them had been quietly religious young men whose faith had been shaken by their involvement in the War. After seeing their childhood homes razed to the ground by German bombers or their fellow soldiers being slain on the beaches of Normandy, they had slowly and unwillingly concluded that God was not merely dead but had probably never lived. The resulting sense of ideological hunger was well-nigh unbearable. Desperate to replace their threadbare Christianity with a sturdier

Weltanschauung, many of them had shopped around in the unlikeliest byways of modern thought. An eccentric carpenter called Jack embraced the free-market individualism of Herbert Spencer and spent six confused months studying *Social Statics*. A slightly pompous civil servant called Joe, noted for his fur hats and his supercilious way of speaking, spent an enraptured evening with *The Rubaiyat of Omar Khayyam* and described himself thereafter as a 'bibulous pagan'. Some of the more pious types even made a last-ditch effort to retain their spirituality, exploring Buddhist, Hindu and Muslim texts in search of an irrefutable argument for the existence of God. But none of this had lasted. What had rescued these decent and intelligent men from their disorientation was the Communist Party.

Their Marxism was indelibly shaped by the politics of the Popular Front. They had all joined the Party before the end of the War, when communists still believed that the defence of democracy was more important than the struggle for socialism. 'We were anything but sectarian', as Bob told me one night over a glass of lemonade in a half-empty pub. 'We knew that fascism posed a grave threat to the workers and that our first priority was to smash it, even if we had to unite with liberals, conservatives and other people from the right.' It was a lesson they never forgot. In the long years since the defeat of Hitler their faith in democracy had been tested and tested again and never found wanting. They had always insisted that socialism would only succeed if it built on the achievements of 'bourgeois liberalism'. The Soviet Union meant very little to them and was often dismissed, usually in a despairing aside, as a blot on the political landscape. What really drove them forward was the sense that freedom of speech, individual liberty and the rule of law would finally come into their own once capitalism had been swept aside. I already knew from bitter experience that not everyone on the left felt the same.

The truly seminal moments in life are those which leave one stimulated and chastened in equal measure. Not everything about my early meetings with Swansea's communists was a liberation. The more I heard those magnificently earnest old men analyse the 'current situation' or talk about their eclectic intellectual interests, the more I had to face up to the depths of my own ignorance. It was becoming clear that my exiguous knowledge of Marxism would have to be sharpened up. Faced with a group of war veterans who knew Western civilisation more intimately than their own children, I could no longer win an argument by peppering my sentences with references to 'class struggle', 'capitalist crisis' or 'imperialist war'. It was time to find out what those talismanic phrases actually meant. For several weeks I felt strangely unsettled by a gnawing sense of intellectual dissatisfaction. In some obscure way I realised that I was building up to a moment of transfiguration – a moment of feverish, self-absorbed cerebrality that would change my angle of vision forever. I didn't know it at the time but thousands of men and women from Bombay to Moscow and London to Addis Ababa had taken the same path in the years gone by. I was about to embark on my first encounter with the Marxist classics.

The hour of knowledge eventually struck on a grey Wednesday afternoon in the late spring. I had returned home early from the dire college of further education in which I was pretending to do my 'A' levels. At about four o' clock, flicking distractedly through that month's copy of *Marxism Today*, I decided to catch the bus to the university bookshop. My plan was to buy an anthology of writings by Marx and Engels, one of the many thick Marxist tomes that stood on the Politics shelves in those long-lost days when the USSR still existed and Trotskyists presided over every common room. At this point my head was filled with the most ludicrous intellectual fantasies. Gazing out of the window as the bus made its way along the chilly coastal road towards the university campus, I reckoned that if I made good progress with the book I could acquire all the knowledge I needed in about three weeks. Little did I know.

As soon as I got home I had to chew my way impatiently through one of my mother's lamb casseroles. After the last runner bean was eaten I excused myself from the table, sat with my back against the bureau in my room and began to read. Like everything published by Progress Publishers in Moscow, my copy of *The Selected Works of Karl Marx and Frederick Engels in One Volume* was very badly produced. The pages were as thin as tissue paper, the print as minuscule as a colony of baby gnats and the spine as sturdy as custard. But that was all for the good. The book's extreme lack of elegance prepared me for the new phase I was about to enter. It made it clear that from now on I would be reading for enlightenment and not for pleasure or entertainment. The first thing I looked at was Marx's 'Preface' to *A Contribution to the Critique of Political Economy* (1859), one of the most heavily cited documents in the whole of human history. Here was my first real exposure to the Marxist theory of how societies develop. Three sentences in particular seemed to hum with significance:

> In the social production of their life, men enter into definite relations that are indispensable and independent of their will, relations of production which correspond to a definite stage of development of their material productive forces. The sum total of these relations of production constitutes the economic structure of society, the real foundation, on which rises a legal and political superstructure and to which correspond definite forms of social consciousness. The mode of production of material life conditions the social, political and intellectual life process in general. It is not the consciousness of men that determines their being, but, on the contrary, their social being that determines their consciousness.[41]

41 Karl Marx and Frederick Engels, *Selected Works in One Volume* (London: Lawrence and Wishart, 1980), p. 181.

As I scanned these lines I experienced a sudden inrush of comprehension. For twenty or thirty minutes I allowed myself to believe that history was as clear as spring water. All the causes and the connections, the motive forces and the overarching relationships were magically laid bare. So that's what it was all about! In my mind's eye I saw a succession of labouring men and the 'material forces of production' that had shaped their very different worlds. In a few phantasmagoric seconds I saw a hunter gatherer with his spear and a peasant with his hoe and a cloth-capped proletarian at his factory bench. And there, hovering above them like tiers on a wedding cake, I saw all the things that persuaded them to keep working – the laws, the ideas, the soldiers and the politicians. It turned out that the chaos of experience was not so chaotic after all. The accuracy of Marx's ideas was of no concern to me. All that mattered was that centuries of human endeavour had been fed through a theoretical prism and emerged in the form of a neatly labelled diagram. The economy was the base and everything else was the superstructure. New forms of technology remade the base in their own image. The base determined the superstructure but sometimes the superstructure influenced the base. In a fit of intellectual déjà vu I was seized by the belief that I had known these things all along. It felt as if a capsule of historical insight had been lying dormant in my brain, waiting to be fertilised by the right text. The past belonged to me.

It is hard to look back on those brief moments of lucidity without feeling slightly ill. Even before the evening was out I'd realised that things weren't as simple as I'd assumed. The questions crowded in on me like cawing blackbirds. How exactly did the forces of production determine the relations of production? In what sense did the superstructure correspond to the base? And what did all this have to do with socialism? If I'd known what was coming next I might well have abandoned my studies for good. Instead I screwed up my courage, glanced nervously at the mountains of knowledge in front of me and set off from the foothills of my own ignorance for the last time.

The most *agonistic* relationship of my life – the relationship with the history of thought – had begun in earnest. For a few months I read so obsessively that I felt like a pious monk being ritually flayed. Every synapse in my brain howled with tension as I struggled to understand what I was reading. After coming to terms with Marx and Engels (and let me say it now: Frederick Engels was one of the greatest exegetes who ever lived), I sweated and puzzled and underlined my way through Lenin, Stalin and Mao. Soon I was burying myself in immense single-volume histories of Philosophy, Sociology and Economics. Scholarly works on the development of socialism (and on my favourite subject – the history of the Communist Party) were bolted down in the luminous dawns and the heavy, windswept nights. If Marxism was a philosophy of everything, I had no choice but to stay awake until the universe had yielded its secrets.

Whenever someone asked me to explain my passion for books – a passion so sudden and immoderate that it struck many of my friends as pure affectation – I replied with a pompous little speech about the political responsibilities of Marxists. Only the erudite could aspire to change the world, or so I liked to proclaim. Sometimes I went so far as to quote Lenin, whose absurdly grandiloquent dictum about the need for constant studying I'd taken care to commit to memory: 'Communism becomes an empty phrase, a mere façade, and a communist a mere bluffer, if he has not worked over in his consciousness the whole inheritance of human knowledge.'[42] Yet even at the time I distrusted my own motives. In my heart I knew that my hunger for knowledge wasn't entirely untainted by egotism. How could it have been? After a lifetime of embarrassing educational failure, I cherished the idea that my approach to scholarship was somehow more *authentic* than that of my contemporaries. If the stellar performers in the Sixth Form were only interested in getting into Oxbridge, or so I liked to tell myself, I pursued the life of the mind for rather nobler reasons. At some level I

42 Quoted in Robert Sullivan, *Christopher Caudwell* (London: Croom Helm, 1987), p. 39.

truly believed that my desire to know everything was a spiritual one. My goal was to recreate the whole of human history in my own mind, imbuing it with a coherence, a dignity and a sheer aesthetic grandeur that it hadn't possessed in reality. As absurd as it now seems, I conceived of adult life as a sort of endless vista of visions. In the future I would retreat inwards at will and luxuriate in an enchanted landscape of learning. Others could ply their trivial trades or indulge their vulgar passions but I would converse with Plato, watch in awe as Leonardo wielded his hammer or thrill to the sight of the Winter Palace being stormed. Today I can hardly recall these beautiful adolescent dreams without crying. In the end it was the bedazzled Keats, not the crudely practical Lenin, who spoke for my soul: 'Knowledge enormous makes a God of me'.[43]

My exorbitant ambitions were reinforced by the circumstances in which my early studies took place. By the 1980s an entire generation of socialist militants was dying off. The men and women who discovered Marxism in the period between the wars were slowly expiring under the weight of old age, hard work and political disappointment. One of the results was that the second-hand bookshops started to overflow with their old books. In Ralph the Books on Dillwyn Street there was a revolving stand that towered to the ceiling with 'recent acquisitions'. Nearly every week its display of socialist literature from forty, fifty or sixty years ago was replenished. At one stage it became so important to my education that I virtually organised my week around it. On Friday mornings in term time, liberated from double English at eleven and with no further lessons until the afternoon, I'd walk down the hill from the college and arrive at the shop at about 11.30. I'd then spend at least half an hour choosing my reading for the next seven days. Orange paperbacks from the Left Book Club, yellowed copies of *Labour Monthly* or *Marxist Quarterly*, odd volumes from the Thinker's Library and bombastic philosophical tomes from Stalin's Russia

43 'Knowledge enormous makes a God of me' is the 113th line in Book 3 of Keats's 'Hyperion'.

– everything was grist to my autodidactic mill. Rarely paying more than a pound for a single item, I'd laugh meekly at the statutory political joke from the old man behind the counter ('Stalin this week, is it?') and head off to Castle Gardens for a lunchtime read. Sitting there on a park bench with my prawn sandwich from Marks and Spencer and my theoretical tract by Marx and Engels, I suspect I cut a rather pathetic figure.

The point is not that the death of old socialists enabled me to compile a library on the cheap. The point is that I suddenly felt part of an intellectual tradition. Whenever I opened one of those books for the first time I felt a curious sense of looking history in the face. Scanning the pencilled underlinings and the dense annotations at the side of the page, I marvelled at the thought of the indefatigable men and women who had been there before me. These were not the books of intellectuals or academics but of ordinary workers whose greatest desire was to understand. Most of them were miners or factory hands or gardeners who went out to work in the freezing mornings, returned home in the blustery nights and spent all their spare time in the empire of print. Even today their carefully inscribed names on the title pages seem like tokens from a more serious world: Dai Minty, Geoff Hughes, I.J. James. In my more impressionable moments I felt that their intellectual energy still hovered in the air. If I failed to understand something (and no reader of the Marxist classics was ever as obtuse and bovine as I was), I took courage from the thought that my predecessors had struggled long and hard and eventually been able to say 'Yes – I think I grasp it now'. There were times when the experience was almost mediumistic. Turning away in despair from a difficult text and silently appealing to its long-dead owner for help, I would sometimes discover that my temples had ceased to ache and that the words on the page glowed with clarity. As a strict materialist I scoffed at the idea that Dai Minty or some other discarnate communist had answered my prayers. But still the spirits spoke.

———

If the Communist Party inducted me into the religion of books, it also scoured my soul with self-doubt. In my early days in the Party I experienced the fear of fraudulence for the first time. I can still remember the torture of waking in the middle of the night, trying desperately to fabricate a sense of calm and then surrendering in despair as a single insistent question thrust itself into my mind: 'Who do you think you are?' I could scarcely believe that anyone else in the world was as presumptuous as I was. The gap between my capabilities and my ambitions seemed as wide as the Sargasso Sea. There I was, the none-too-thoughtful veteran of a thousand scholastic disasters. How dare I suppose that the worlds of politics, philosophy and literature were mine to master? At my lowest ebb my feelings of self-abnegation were positively Gandhian in their magnitude. More than once I concluded that the wisest thing to do was to renounce my quest for knowledge, donate my books to Oxfam and accept that only the dazzlingly gifted – the sort of people who didn't fail Chemistry O level – could ever be at home in the palaces of the mind. I would simply have to make do with a mess of cultural pottage.

Salvation came from an unlikely source. The time has finally come to tell you about Linda, the terrifying spectre who sold me *The British Road to Socialism* and invited me to my first Party meeting. It was she more than anyone else who taught me that the universe of scholarship has room for everyone. If I'm to explain why, I have to tell you about her extraordinary contradictions. Linda was at one and the same time an immensely cultured woman and a boorish, uncivilised harridan. Those of us who knew her well marvelled at her erudition, her inexhaustible fluency and her love of literature, music and nature. To the rest of the world she seemed less balanced and certainly less cultivated than the tramps in Castle Gardens. Nearly all her associates on the Swansea left would cross the road rather than speak to her, terrified at what might happen to their precious reputations if anyone saw them with this scrofulous denizen of the lower depths. She was the kind of woman who howled obscenities at teenagers in the street, belched loudly in public meetings and spoke with scholarly exactitude about religion in prehistory or narrative structure in the novels of Jane Austen. I have often thought that only the language of Lévi-Strauss can do her justice. Quite simply, Linda united the best of culture and the worst of nature in a single astonishing package.

Perhaps I should start again. This is not a matter that can be dispatched in a single paragraph. The point about Linda is that you can only appreciate her gifts if you've had some experience of her ghastliness. The first instinct of anyone who talks about her is to veer wildly between the descriptive and the anecdotal. The desire to evoke her frightful appearance rapidly gives way to appalled recollections of her improbable exploits. When I first met her there was a lot of talk about nuclear war in the air, and it occurred to me fairly early that her stunted body and savagely coarse face were a warning from the future. It was as if some peace-loving deity, intent on scaring humanity out of its drive to war, had shown us what men and women might look like after nuclear weapons had ravaged the earth. She was less than five-feet tall and bludgeoned her way forwards on bowed legs and inturned feet. Her back was arched and people sometimes compared her to Quasimodo. Her skin was sallow, her mouth crooked and her moustache luxuriant. The eyes breathed malignity through large-framed spectacles and a mass of lank hair framed her face like two sheaves of diseased corn. Everything about Linda's appearance betrayed the depths of her mental suffering. She was famous among connoisseurs of the grotesque throughout the city. She was the place where genes went to die.

Anecdotes? I've got thousands of them. Linda's behaviour has long been a byword for sheer unconquerable brutishness. The frightening thing about her explosions of incivility is that they seem to rear up from her inner depths. One gets the impression that her brain is connected directly to her bowels and that a disturbance in the latter immediately calls forth anarchy in the former. How else to explain her window-rattling outbursts of rage, her witheringly obscene language and her shameless lack of manners? I swear that the following example has not been improved in the telling.

At the height of the Miners' Strike, Linda and her friend Barbara Fischer organised a jumble sale for the NUM at a local church hall. The vicar did not support the union but put the hall at its disposal in a spirit of Christian charity. On the morning in question he turned up early, chatted amiably with Barbara and expressed the hope that things were going well. As Barbara thanked him for his generosity, she glanced over his shoulder and saw Linda launching into an argument with a weedy young activist from the SWP.[44] 'Please God', she said to herself, 'let the vicar leave before Linda starts a war'. The apocalypse unfolded with biblical speed. In a matter of seconds Linda had dragged the Trotskyist across the floor and shoved him into the vicar's line of vision. Then, in her appallingly stentorian way – a friend of mine once described her voice as 'a cross between a foghorn and a fart' – she urged her comrade to have the final word: 'Barbara!', she boomed, 'Will you tell this fucking cunt that he's talking *complete fucking shit*!'

One more for the road. There was one occasion when Linda turned up unexpectedly at my family home to retrieve a book I'd borrowed from her. It was a quiet Sunday morning and the neighbourhood was plunged in wintry silence. We ushered our guest into the lounge and offered her a cup of coffee and a biscuit. The coffee was gratefully accepted but the biscuit prompted a brisk lecture on dietetics. Fixing my mother with a look of undisguised exasperation, Linda explained that she'd had a bowl of porridge and an apple for breakfast and that anything else would be excessive: 'I can't understand people who poison their bodies with sugary muck'. Her reference to the body must have had a galvanising effect on her digestive processes, since immediately afterwards she asked to be shown to the toilet. Within seconds of shutting the door the nature of her intentions

44 It almost goes without saying that Linda used to refer to the SWP as the 'shit, wind and piss brigade'.

became clear. The toilet was at least thirty feet away from the lounge but the acoustics in our house have always been very good. Stunned into immobility by the Rabelaisian nature of our fate, my parents and I sat there with grey faces as a succession of staccato farts, agonised sighs and resounding plops assailed our ears. This was biology in the service of domestic terrorism.

Once Linda had ambled off down the road we realised that a cloud of radioactive matter was advancing towards us down the corridor. Deploying the air freshener with all the zeal of an early puritan reformer, my mother looked on the bright side: 'At least we know where she left her porridge', she observed.

But enough of all that. Like most of the oddities, loners and eccentrics who roam the streets of British cities, Linda seems to exist in a place where the laws of history have no purchase. She gives the impression of having arrived in the world fully formed and of being much the same today as she always has been and always will be. Yet over the years the bare facts of her past have slowly trickled out. She was born soon after the outbreak of the War to severely impoverished parents in Hereford. I have heard people make dark noises about the treatment she received at the hands of her father, but I suspect their remarks owe more to contemporary anxieties than to the true course of her life. What we know for sure is that she left school at a very young age and immediately became a 'skivvy' (her own word) for a wealthy family. This stage of her existence still looms in her memory with a sort of Dickensian horror. For nearly twenty years she cleaned the floors, ran errands to the town, cooked the food and washed the dishes and cowered under the lash of her employer's sarcasm. When it came – and it seems to have come as suddenly as a clap of thunder in a clear sky – her break with what she calls the 'old world' required more courage than most of us will ever be able to muster. One morning she simply got out of bed, packed her pitifully sparse belongings in a rucksack and caught the bus to North Wales. Within a week she'd enrolled on an adult learners' course at a local college. Within five years she'd taken a brilliant degree at Cardiff University and given the local

Communist Party a savage kick to its corpulent rear. Her move to Swansea came soon after that.

There is no other way of putting it: Linda was *saved* by Marxism. In her first term at Cardiff she became obsessed with the Marxist classics, recognising – or so I like to surmise – that they gave her the knowledge she needed to draw a line under her years of domestic servitude. The world that had treated her so badly was now comprehensible in all its obscurest details. There was no hint of personal ambition in her decision to join the Party. For much of the last forty years she has lived off benefits and carved a reputation as the most selfless, the most maddening and the most *indefatigable* activist in South Wales. What keeps her going is the desire to free herself from the memory of her own suffering. In her heart she believes that the socialist future will redeem her miserable past. When the milk of plebeian kindness flows freely and man is no longer beast to man, History will at last have taken its revenge on the affluent, cultured and savage couple who made her scrub the floors until her bones ached.

The obverse side of her boorishness is an extraordinary sense of delicacy. I will always remember visiting her at her tatty council flat on a dispiriting New Year's Eve towards the end of the 1980s. It was bitterly cold and the pale afternoon sun was setting over the rooftops. Sitting together in her unlit living room, Linda and I swapped a few banalities about the state of the world as a recording of Sibelius's *Finlandia* swelled around us. Slowly but surely the music lulled us into silence. Crepuscular violins traced out exquisite arches in the air. The percussion rumbled and churned like the distant sea. When I glanced across I saw that Linda had her eyes closed and that her mouth was twitching slightly in an intimation of subdued ecstasy. There was nothing affected about it. At that moment the snows of Finland were more real to her than the squalor of her flat, the poverty of her neighbourhood or the melancholy of the turning year. Here was a woman in the grip of a vision. Because I was not yet at an age when significant experiences were their own reward, I remember telling myself that this was Marxist civilisation at its most luminous: 'Under communism, everyone will be like this'.

Let me spell out my debt to Linda as plainly as I can. No one else has taught me so much about pursuing the life of the mind in impropitious circumstances. Cranky, poverty-stricken and more than a little unstable, utterly incapable of behaving thoughtfully or sustaining a proper friendship, Linda is nevertheless the most cultured person I know. She has never doubted for a second that the 'best that has been thought and said' (a phrase of Matthew Arnold's that she cherishes) is hers to possess. Her creed is an utterly democratic one: The myriad worlds of literature, history, music, philosophy, politics, science and art are the property of Everyman. Anyone who tells you otherwise is denying you your birthright. By following her example I began to realise that I too needed no invitation to open the library door.

I had better make a confession. I haven't been entirely honest about the role of Mother Russia. So far I've given the impression that I loathed the USSR and that the communists I knew in Swansea were largely indifferent to it. But things were always more complicated than that. The plain truth is that the Soviet Union functioned in our lives like a smouldering devil on all our shoulders. The more we tried to ignore it – the more we reminded ourselves that the world's first workers' state had viciously betrayed its founding ideals – the more urgently and the more seductively it whispered in our ears. 'Don't believe all those bourgeois lies!', or so it seemed to tell us. 'The Soviet motherland is a place of peace and plenty and your duty is to support it at whatever the cost!' Some of us were more immune to this sort of thing than others: I'm not being dishonest when I say that I was more immune to it than most. Yet the fact remains that those of us who considered ourselves anti-Soviet were always half in love with the thing we opposed.

My public position on the USSR was simple enough, even

if it bordered a bit too much on Trotskyism for some of my friends in the Party. Knowing all too well about the endless food queues, the scandalous absence of basic liberties and the wretched history of mass murder, I argued that the Soviet Union was a socialist country in name only. It was true that the means of production had long since been nationalised and that the potential of the system was enormous, yet it was equally clear that socialism would never work properly without a drastic infusion of democracy. What was needed was a 'political revolution' that would devolve power away from the Kremlin towards the common people. Playfully adapting Lenin's famous aphorism, I took to saying that 'Public ownership + democratic rights = Communism'.[45] Where I differed from the Trotskyists was in my assessment of how the revolution would be made. My acquaintances in Militant or the IMG said that Stalinism could only be galvanised into life by a mass uprising. By contrast, I put an enormous and utterly risible amount of faith in the Soviet Communist Party. For a few years I seriously believed that the lean-faced sages at the top of the government – those forbidding and cruel men with their heavy overcoats, their silver hair and their blank expressions – would awake one day and suddenly decide to give away their own power. In an essay I wrote in university in 1987, I claimed that Mikhail Gorbachev was an 'instinctive democrat' whose programme of *glasnost* and *perestroika* would finally realise the sweet fantasies of October. Some of my other predictions were even more accurate.

On the whole I'm not embarrassed by any of this. I wasn't the only person who thought that 'actually existing socialism' might one day be reformed for the better, nor did I ever pretend that the USSR was anything other than a pretty ghastly place. What *does* make me uncomfortable when I look back on it is my attitude to Soviet culture. I joined the Communist Party when the world was embroiled in what some people called the 'second Cold War'. Europe seemed to be divided down the middle into

45 In his report to the Seventh Congress of the Soviet Communist Party in 1920, Lenin famously observed that 'Communism is Soviet power plus the electrification of the whole country.'

two homogeneous blocs, one defined by the bright pageant of consumerism and the other by the greyer textures of Russian solemnity. My abiding sin was to imagine – or at least to suspect – that the culture of the socialist camp was superior to that of the West. When I thought about life in Moscow or Leningrad (or for that matter in East Berlin or Bucharest), I took it for granted that totalitarianism had imbued everyday affairs with an awesome seriousness. I couldn't imagine the thousands of people in the fields, factories and offices behaving frivolously. Governed by a humourless *nomenklatura* that had frightened them into political docility, they had surely retreated inwards in a determined quest for self-cultivation. In my mind's eye I saw them poring over cheap editions of Tolstoy, struggling to master foreign languages or exulting at the sight of a lone crow soaring above snowbound fields. The West could boast its endless display of tacky treasures but the Soviet people had been *oppressed into wisdom.*

All this is easy enough to explain, of course. My delusions about socialist culture were a direct expression of the ascetic streak that had always beleaguered me. Still half-attracted and half-terrified by the overweening hedonism of my own society, I consoled myself with the thought that life was lived more seriously over the horizon. The thing that troubles me in retrospect is the realisation that my taste for the ascetic – my yearning for what I once called 'buried and dusty places' – was shaped by some pretty unhealthy impulses. This is a matter that I can best approach indirectly. At the beginning of my time in the Party I was very interested in the 'official' Soviet art of the Stalin period. Even with my shamefully untutored eye I realised that Socialist Realism had very little going for it, but for a few months I gorged myself on those absurdly stylised portraits of collective farms, Stakhanovite workers and heroic leaders in which Soviet artists specialised. After a while I noticed something peculiar: A very high proportion of the paintings incorporated large stretches of canvas that were more or less devoid of detail. One of my favourite examples was Tatyana Yablonskaya's *Bread* (1949), a sentimental rendering of agricultural labour whose foreground was largely taken up with a vast expanse of gleaming corn. More striking still was George Nissky's *The Landscape* (1951), which looked for all the world as if the artist had run low on paint and was trying to economise on its use. Ostensibly focused on the signal box of a provincial railway station, its real subject was the immensely gloomy and featureless sky that towered above it. The remarkable thing about these paintings was that their appeal was essentially abstract. After a few viewings their figurative content seemed to recede into the distance and get swallowed up by their wide open spaces.[46]

These days I think I understand what the artists were trying to achieve. By creating an immensity of nothingness at the heart of the picture plane, they were encouraging the viewer to project his own meanings, fantasies or preoccupations onto their vision of Soviet society. In stark contrast to their reputation for out-and-out Stalinism, Nissky, Yablonskaya and a host of other painters had a strikingly *dialogic* understanding of socialist art. They believed that the purpose of their work was to provide a space in which the diktats of the Soviet government could meld unpredictably with the deepest wishes of the individual citizen. As a teenager I understood none of this. In fact my response to Soviet paintings was more about avoiding effort than promoting it. As self-conscious as any other adolescent who strains to appreciate high culture, I often sat at my desk with a bright light pointing directly at a photograph of *Bread*, *The Landscape* or some other favourite. Almost invariably I tried to relax my eyes until the featureless stretches of the paintings anaesthetised my field of vision. The effect was a curiously miasmic one. Sitting there with a vague impression of nirvana playing across my optic nerves, I sometimes felt that nothing could be nicer than to surrender to oblivion with an unfrightened heart. It was all a bit of a paradox. My membership of the Communist Party had gone a long way towards tempering my laziness, proving that

46 *Bread* and *The Landscape* are both reproduced in Gleb Prokhorov, *Art Under Socialist Realism: Soviet Painting 1930-1950* (Roseville East, NSW: Craftsman House, 1995).

a life without intellectual or political effort was no life at all. It had certainly cured me of my belief that working people were workshy and irresponsible. Yet those blissed-out sessions at my desk clearly pointed backwards to the fecklessness I had once embraced. My victory over the death impulse was by no means complete. At some level of my mind I still aspired to luxuriate in a void.

But that's as far as my Russophilia went. My guilty fascination with the dark heart of Soviet culture never translated itself into political sympathy. If I ever felt tempted to adopt a pro-Soviet position, I only had to think about the more encrusted 'Tankies' in the Swansea Branch and the urge would quickly pass.[47] In my day the Party's pro-Soviet faction was relatively small and palpably on the wrong side of history. A few of its members were sweet-natured pensioners whose only real sin was chronic sentimentality, but most of the rest were ghastly beyond endurance. In general they fell into one of two categories. Quite a few of them were clearly suffering from a species of emotional desperation. Feeling rejected or at least not adequately appreciated in their own society, they buttressed their fragile egos by telling themselves that everything would have been different in the USSR. Their most salient characteristic was the ferocity of their historical revisionism. Determined not to betray the one society that might have taken them to its heart, they were incapable of admitting that anything bad had ever happened there. As late as 1995, four years after the Soviet Communist Party had been turfed out of the Kremlin in utter ignominy, one of them told me that Russia was still 'essentially socialist' because its 'planned economy has proved too efficient to be dismantled'. There was a look in his eyes which implored me not to disagree with him. If the motherland no longer existed then his heart must surely break.

The other bunch of Tankies were less pathetic but much more sinister. These were the people who not only acknowledged the

47 The so-called 'Tankies' in the Communist Party were unreconstructed Stalinists who acquired their souhriquet because of their support for the Soviet invasion of Czechoslovakia in 1968.

horrors of Soviet history but positively revelled in them. In any discussion of the Gulag, the Great Purges or the Molotov-Ribbentrop Pact, their faces would twitch with malice as they patiently explained that socialist omelettes can only be made after capitalist eggs have been cracked. Their logic was simple. Since capitalist society is brutal, it behoves revolutionaries to be more brutal still. Only someone who feels no mercy towards the class enemy – someone who exults in the thought of cutting a banker's throat and feeding his children to the sharks – can ever be relied upon to free the people from their torment. What they never seemed to realise was that their bloodlust had robbed them of the qualities that brought them into politics in the first place. Nearly all of them dismissed compassion, anger at injustice or the desire for more freedom as instances of 'bourgeois idealism'. Their monstrous self-regard was rooted solely in their appetite for violence, in their unshakeable belief that no one else saw life as honestly and unsentimentally as they did. I once asked a Stalinist civil servant whether he fantasised about shooting his political enemies when he lay in bed at night. The only response he could muster was 'Now that's just *silly*, comrade', but the look in his eyes conveyed a different message. He would have killed me if he could.

CHAPTER 6
Breakdown

It was somewhere between three and four in the morning on a cold autumn weekday. I woke with a start and immediately registered the pressure on my bladder. That last cup of tea had clearly been a mistake. After pulling on my dressing gown and sidestepping a pile of books on the floor (the mere sight of Jean-François Lyotard's *The Postmodern Condition* was enough to make me wince), I left my room and descended uncertainly to the bathroom on the second floor. My landlady's taste was execrable. The tiles on the wall were a chilly combination of black and silver, the window was covered with *art nouveau* transfers and the toilet had a purple seat. I turned on the light above the mirror and stared at my reflection for at least twenty seconds. There was nothing pretty about it. The only thing worse than the hollow cheeks, the parchment-pale skin and the lank hair was the hint of vacancy in my eyes. I looked as bad as I felt. As I inhaled deeply and ran my tongue around a broken tooth, I asked myself a question that seemed to emerge from the depths of my being: 'Why did I ever believe that I could understand the world?'

I remember the moment so clearly because it was the start of a season in hell. I was a few months short of my twenty-second birthday and in my first term as a postgraduate researcher at an English university. On the face of it my prospects looked good. Earlier in the year I'd completed an improbable transition from pathetic dunce to budding scholar, earning a first-class degree without noticeably exerting myself. There was a feeling among my friends that I would acquire a PhD by the time I was twenty-five and proceed to a career as an academic. Most of my tutors seemed to agree, bandying around terms like 'clever', 'highly sophisticated' and 'aesthetically and exegetically gifted' whenever they discussed my work. Even my Greek girlfriend, an ambitious and talented young lawyer who tended to speak English in italics, told me everyday that '*You have to become a Professor!*' If other people's confidence in me had been a sufficient condition of success, I'd never have looked back.

In fact I was heading straight for the edge of a cliff. To use a simile of William Styron's, I felt – or rather my brain felt – like a telephone exchange slowly being submerged in water.[48] Nothing made sense. I had lost the ability to understand even the simplest ideas. Whenever I tried to do some reading – and I opened dozens of books every week in the hope that one of them would spark my recovery – I found myself weighed down by the most crippling feelings of self-consciousness. Estranged from the storehouse of intuition on which genuine understanding is based, I stared at the words on the page so despairingly that their meaning simply drifted away. My command of language was seriously under threat. Although my spoken English was still tolerably fluent, I couldn't write a decent sentence to save my life. I was probably the only doctoral candidate in the country whose pages sounded so amateurish. One memorably awful afternoon, thumbing through a local newspaper while eating lunch in a burger bar, I came across a letter to the editor written by a twelve-year-old girl from a nearby school. It was clear, witty and eloquent. I realised with a shudder that I simply couldn't match it.

Many things were responsible for the zomboid state in which I found myself. Deficient brain chemistry, scanty self-confidence and a lack of common sense all played their part. But at the heart of the problem were the ideological obsessions that had drawn me towards scholarship in the first place. When I first went to university I thought that my premature immersion in Marxism

48 William Styron, *Darkness Visible: A Memoir of Madness* (London: Jonathan Cape, 1991), pp. 47-48.

gave me an advantage over my fellow students. Now I realised that it had come close to ruining me. In part it was a matter of excessive ambition. Having thrown in my lot at a very young age with an ideology that purported to explain everything, I felt a keen obligation to explore as many academic disciplines as I could. The problem was that I had neither the intellectual commitment nor the self-discipline to see my plans through. For three years as an undergraduate I buzzed around like a blue-arsed fly from one subject to another, acquiring a smattering of knowledge from each but never staying long enough to sink deep roots. No graduate in History and Philosophy ever knew as little of those disciplines as I did, or so it sometimes seemed. I often told myself that my success was solely due to exceptionally generous marking, a certain intellectual liveliness and a towering capacity to bullshit. Erudite I was not.

My other difficulty was that Marxism had turned me into a species of methodological fanatic. Massively deluded about the extent of my historical knowledge, I felt compelled to 'apply' Marxism to everything I came across. The result was that I could never respond to an idea on its own terms. Faced with the structuralist theory of language, Heidegger's notion of *Dasein* or Lacan's reformulation of psychoanalysis (to name just three of the things which tormented me during that first postgraduate year), I rarely gave myself enough time to appreciate what they were all about. Instead I immediately posed the questions that I thought a Marxist would be expected to pose. In what social circumstances did these ideas arise? Whose material interests did they serve? How did they relate to other aspects of the dominant ideology of the day? How would they be regarded in the socialist society of the future? After wrestling with these conundrums for five or ten minutes I often got the feeling that both hemispheres of my brain had filled with concrete. Every last glimmer of comprehension was buried underfoot. I had always prided myself on my powers of empathy, but sitting there at my desk – head bowed, hands arched, eyes scrunched with concentration – I could no more commune with the great thinkers of the past than fly out of the window by flapping my arms. The great love of my life had let me down. Marxism was no longer a penetrating light but a sweltering straitjacket that cut me off from the world outside. I had no idea where I was going.

A more balanced person might have realised that the crisis would pass. But common sense has never been my strong suit. As I fretted continuously over my lack of cerebral muscle, I allowed my mind to set deeper and deadlier traps for me. Suddenly I could barely cope with the simplest aspects of everyday life. Like one of those mumbling schizophrenics one occasionally sees on the street – unshaven, self-absorbed, palpably without hope – I began to ascribe metaphysical significance to my thoughts. I became possessed by the idea that if an impure, complacent or vengeful image passed across my mind, some catastrophic event would occur shortly afterwards. Merely to think about illness or death or disfigurement was to invite the real thing to inflict itself upon me. The only way to contain the insurgent power of my own mind was to follow the path of ritual. Prayer became the main currency of my existence. Within seconds of the unwanted thoughts rearing upwards, I clasped my hands together and implored God the Father to forgive me. It was not unusual for my stock phrases to be repeated five or ten times. Sometimes I buttressed the prayer with a preposterous but precisely calibrated routine, rearranging ornaments on the mantelpiece or stepping back and forth across a threshold until all my energy was spent. The anguish seared through my skull like an electric current through water. The hideous oscillations between obsession and compulsion took up all my time. The hour of religious mania was upon me.

The people who were closest to me knew that something was wrong but rarely voiced their concerns for fear of causing offence. It was only a deeply eccentric High Anglican called Rowan – the gnarled veteran of a thousand deep and meaningful conversations – who had some inkling of what I was going through. One evening he spoke with *ex cathedra* fluency about what he preeningly called the 'aetiology' of my illness. 'It's obviously got something to do with Marxism', or so he told me. 'I've known all along that you're the sort of person who experiences deep religious impulses from an early age. The complicating factor in your case is that your hunger for the divine scares the shit out of you and you've spent your life trying to suppress it. You embraced Marxism so enthusiastically because at some level of your mind you saw it as a substitute religion. As long as you worshipped at the shrine of Father Karl – as long as you convinced yourself that communism would usher in the earthly paradise – you were able to hold your spiritual needs at bay. Now your love affair with Marxism is over and the old desires come bursting through. Just accept it, Philip: Your only option is to try and see God face to face.'

At the time I thought Rowan was talking utter codswallop, though I wasn't heartless enough to tell him so. In retrospect I'm inclined to credit him with half a point. All that stuff about deep religious impulses wasn't true but it gestured towards something real. From a very young age I'd been immensely superstitious, fearing that every impure thought could be heard by an omniscient deity to whom I otherwise paid little attention. Since I associated religion not with joy but with fear, I suppose it's possible that I unconsciously looked around for a system of beliefs that could satiate my spiritual needs without itself being spiritual. Perhaps Marxist theory functioned in my life like an unseen God, conferring meaning on the world by pointing to its coherence, its intelligibility and the possibility that one day everyone would be redeemed. But the problem with Rowan's theory was that it tried to explain too much. Demented with cosmic paranoia, I still knew perfectly well that secular ideologies usually answer to secular needs. Rather like George Bernard Shaw – a colossal genius to whom I don't otherwise presume to compare myself – I knew that I'd opted for socialism because I craved a sense of having some 'business in the world'. The search for a substitute God was at most a secondary issue. Nor did I care for the suggestion that my problems could only be solved by abandoning politics and embracing religion. In the depths of my confusion I sensed the need for a third way – one which balanced the secular and the spiritual, the material and the ethical and the here and now with the world hereafter. For a long time my sense of higher powers interfering in my daily life was too insistent, too starkly terrifying to allow me to believe that I would ever be free of it. I assumed that my religious burden would be with me for the rest of my life. My goal was to render it tolerable by sublimating it in political struggle. I had been active in the Communist Party for three years but then drifted away as my problems mounted. Now I began to feel that a return to the left was my only hope. In the great tradition of Edward Carpenter, Joseph Needham and Conrad Noel – three thinkers whose synthesis of Christianity and socialism I had once dismissed as flaky – I vowed to become the sort of revolutionary who kept one eye on the barricades and the other on the greater glory of God. Only then would the voices in my head be stilled.

I wasn't the only person who was plagued by religion as the 1980s drew to a close. Global uncertainty inspired a revival of spiritual feeling in the unlikeliest of places. When I look back on what was undoubtedly one of the worst periods of my life, I cannot help but think that my baroque emotional problems were reinforced – though not fundamentally caused – by the bewildering changes in the world around me. Just think of the landmarks that were washed into the sea while Margaret Thatcher, Ronald Reagan and Mikhail Gorbachev presided over world politics like a triumvirate from Hell. Welfare states, public ownership and strong trade unions – all were swept away during the great neo-liberal *dégringolade*. The socialist countries lost their last traces of dynamism. Fierce mullahs with trailing beards and Kalashnikovs disturbed the peace of the Orient, enticing their followers in Bradford or London to burn books in the name of Allah. In a very real sense the economies of Latin America and Sub-Saharan Africa disappeared altogether. It is hardly surprising that so many people should have looked towards the sky and said 'In God we Trust'. Everything else seemed too impermanent to be worth betting on.

An interest in what was usually called 'spirituality' even trickled down to those of us who were under forty, though no one could agree about the nature of enlightenment or where it might be found. The more adventurous thirtysomethings suddenly became apologists for the 'New Age', earnestly invoking the likes of Jung, Gurdjieff and Ouspensky and signing up for classes in Transcendental Meditation. Among younger people the fashion was for 'rave culture', which seemed to involve dancing sinuously in fields, wearing loose clothes and taking large doses of Ecstasy. As mortifying as it now seems, I was briefly attached to a tiny subculture whose aim was to fuse these trends with Marxism. What follows is a cautionary tale.

Everything began after I drifted back to Swansea in the summer of 1989, profoundly unwell and ready to consign my PhD to the dustbin of history. At the time there was an excellent radical bookshop perched next to a pub towards the far end of Bryn-Y-Môr Road. Run by a cheerful collective of anarchists and named 'Emma's' after Emma Goldman, it served as a meeting place not merely for unreconstructed revolutionaries but also for an eccentric tribe of would-be mystics, radical vegans and holistic therapists. One of its regular customers was a dropout in his late thirties whom a friend and I uncharitably knew as 'Lobbo', on the grounds that only a frontal lobotomy could explain his hair-raising political craziness. I suppose the best way of summing him up is to say that Lobbo was a hippie posing as a Maoist. His appearance and his manner were unashamed throwbacks to the early 1970s. Fatally attracted to phrases such as 'The Man is getting heavy with the people', he had a mane of prematurely grey hair which parted in the middle and cascaded onto his shoulders. His customary uniform was a battered leather jacket, a tie-dyed sweatshirt and a pair of burgundy flares. In spite of all this, he had somehow become involved with an obscure groupuscule which preached the virtues of Maoism and supported 'socialist Albania'. He could often be found in the café at the back of Emma's, sipping camomile tea and quoting slogans from the *Little Red Book*. The word on the street was that Lobbo was a sad acid casualty who should always be treated with caution. So naturally I spoke to him whenever I could.

One sweltering morning in July I turned up early at Emma's and found Lobbo in an excitable mood. Sitting at his usual table in the café with a pile of leaflets in front of him, he saw me come in and called me over with a ear-splitting cry of 'Comrade! Come and have a look at this!' As I sat down he pushed a leaflet across the table and gestured for me to read it. It was printed on light pink paper and had a startling graphic showing a Byzantine icon of Christ emblazoned on a red flag. Across the top in bold letters was the deathless slogan: 'Against Capitalism! Against Spiritual Poverty!' The verbatim form of the relatively short text escapes my memory, but give or take a few exclamation marks it went something like this:

> A new age is upon us. The old barriers between politics and religion are beginning to break down. Large numbers of people are choosing to resist capitalism in the name of the spirit. Angered by the spiritual emptiness of our trivial consumer culture, they become daily more aware that their innate religious needs can only be realised in a socialist society. The purpose of the Jürgen Moltmann Society is to encourage the growth of political and spiritual radicalism in Swansea. If you are interested in joining us in our work, please write for details to The Jürgen Moltmann Society, P.O. Box 69, Swansea.

Lobbo was renowned for producing leaflets and handing them out to bewildered shoppers on the street, but this one clearly wasn't the product of his own erratic hand. Its production values were too high and its language too competent. Smiling beatifically while stroking his beard with nicotine-stained fingers, he explained that he was distributing the leaflets on behalf of a 'wise sannyasin' called Comrade Robert. Based in a terraced house on Hanover Street, Robert was a self-taught exponent of 'messianic Marxism' who had founded the Moltmann Society earlier in the summer.[49] Every week he held meetings for his small group of disciples, most of whom were students at the university. After listening to a lecture on some fairly arcane topic (sample title: 'Was Teilhard's Omega Point a Metaphor for Communism?'), everyone would join together to pray, meditate and perform complex spiritual exercises. The goal was to pursue 'self-actualisation' at the same time as heightening political awareness. 'Why don't you come along?', asked Lobbo. 'The new society will only be born when God and Marx are united.'

I don't want to seem too credulous. I could tell straightaway that The Moltmann Society was likely to be composed of nutters, *soi-disant* messiahs and naive young women. At the same time I couldn't resist the temptation to check it out for myself. I suppose it was a case of a spiritual beggar surveying the blasted landscape all around him, identifying the only available path to redemption and opting through gritted teeth to take it. Crippled by the religious terror that was playing itself out in my head, I longed to see how other people could not merely cope with a sense of the supernatural but actually embrace it. I knew in advance that Robert's lectures would not be a source of enlightenment, but that was hardly the point. What I hoped to get from him was something more important – the example of an intelligent man freely choosing the divine and incorporating it into his everyday life. In a word, I thought he might save me from myself. That's how I came to be sitting in his front room on a warm Tuesday evening.

My first impressions weren't entirely positive. The threadbare curtains had been drawn against the weak evening light and long white candles flickered on the mantelpiece and the hearth. Sticks of incense smouldered in the fireplace but not strongly

49 Almost entirely ignorant of the history of Christian thought, I didn't realise at the time that Moltmann was an important Protestant philosopher and an early exponent of Liberation Theology.

enough to disguise the smell of fish and chips. Each of the three main walls had a single poster at its centre. One depicted a dove of peace (not Picasso's version, which disappointed me slightly), one was a reproduction of Blake's *The Ancient of Days* and the other displayed Albert Korda's famous image of Che Guevara. A recording of Stockhausen's *Kontakte* burbled away to itself in the corner. The atmosphere was more *faux* spiritual than genuinely transcendental. Instructed to sit on the floor by Lobbo, I spent the few minutes before Robert's entrance surreptitiously examining the other attendees. In truth there were only four of us. Apart from Lobbo and a friend of his from the local branch of CND, there was also a distinctive young woman whom I'd occasionally seen at Emma's. Her appearance alone told me that she was part of the rave culture. Small, resoundingly middle-class and bursting with sexual confidence, she wore a loose yellow dress that was sleeveless, *décolletage* and very short. Whenever she moved – sometimes to run her hand through her thick ginger hair, sometimes to scratch the side of her pale but curiously robust face – the Indian bangles on her wrist made a winsome jingling sound. The only sign of out-and-out religiosity was a dayglo image of Christ pinned to the strap of her dress. The thoughts she inspired were profane rather than sacred.

Eventually the door swung open and Robert wafted in, trailing clouds of self-esteem. After making a rueful crack about the low attendance (apparently The Moltmann Society had haemorrhaged 60 per cent of its membership over the previous month), he sat on the floor in the lotus position and began to lecture. His style was very different from that of the secular Marxist orators whose meetings I'd attended so often. In spite of all his talk about overthrowing the rule of Mammon (his title that night was 'Capitalism: The Devil's Own System'), he had little interest in conveying an air of militancy or class-consciousness. His real concern was to leave us in no doubt about the depth of his spiritual gifts. Everything about him seemed to scream 'Attention! Mystic at Work!' Pale and delicate to the point of androgyny, he never looked directly at his audience but stared rapturously above our heads as if conversing with the ghosts of Albion's past. What struck me as particularly creepy was his way of pronouncing things. Horrified by the coarse materiality of the English language, he tried to imbue his sentences with a sort of otherworldly mellifluousness. Every 's' had its sibilance exaggerated ('Jeshush Chrisht shuffered for the peoplesh of the world') and every 't' had its hardness diluted until it sounded more like a 'd'. After quarter of an hour I realised that I'd completely lost track of what was being said. Robert's mannerisms were so unnatural – so redolent with spiritual snobbery – that the ear could hardly withstand them. My mind began to wander.

The fact that I'd taken such an immediate dislike to Robert seemed significant. Almost in an instant it forced me to acknowledge that the goal I'd set myself was ill-advised. The idea that I could recover from religious terror by embracing God more deeply was clearly absurd. My only hope for salvation lay in total blasphemy. I would never be well until every vestige of religion had been chased from my mind and I faced the world as my own master. Sitting there on the floor as Robert wittered on about spiritual essences and astral bodies, I understood more powerfully than ever before why some people loathe authority with every fibre of their being. I was sick to death of the imperious spiritual forces that bade me to obey them at a moment's notice. God wasn't my best friend but my worst enemy. Somehow or other I had to find the strength to stand on my own two feet, shake my fist at the heavens and scream 'Get thee hence, Jehovah' to my worst oppressor. I had no illusions about the difficulty of the challenge in front of me. Even as I vowed to defy the Almighty – even as I aimed a gobbet of figurative spit at Jesus and all his works – my mind caved in once again. The fear of divine wrath sent a shudder of foreboding down my back and I clasped my hands together to pray, hoping that none of the others would notice what I was doing. 'Please forgive me for my disrespectful thoughts', or so I began. 'The path of obedience is hard for the unworthy to follow.'

My prayers only came to an end when Robert concluded his lecture and the second part of the meeting got underway. Seeking to loosen our inhibitions with a benevolent but clearly artificial smile, Robert encouraged us to 'open up' about our problems. Were we experiencing any difficulties in our efforts to achieve a higher form of consciousness? Had we discovered that the path to paradise was bumpier than we thought? If so, the best thing we could do was to 'apply to the Society' for guidance. For twenty or thirty seconds the room was plunged in silence. Lobbo let out a brief phlegmy cough, twitched his nose and stared quizzically at his bootlaces. The guy from CND caught my eye and looked away in a trice, embarrassed by a momentary flicker of intimacy. Then the hiatus was shattered by the girl in the yellow dress. Raising her arm like a child in a classroom, she dilated her eyes flirtatiously and looked towards Robert for permission to speak. 'Emily', he oozed. 'What would you like to share with us?'

It turned out that Emily had been feeling unwell. Faced with all the terrible things in the world – the wars, the poverty, the environmental despoliation – she could no longer find refuge in a personal cocoon of contentment. Her ability to commune with her 'inner child' had disappeared. The world was too much with her. 'It goes without saying that I'm still my own worst enemy', or so she told us in her la-di-da suburban accent. 'I've been working too hard and playing too hard. All week I immerse myself in religious texts and all weekend I party. My intake of drugs is *way* too high. [At the first mention of narcotics, Lobbo chuckled quietly to himself and shot Emily an empathetic grin.] What I need is something to restore my spiritual energies – something to put me back on the straight road of righteousness. Does anyone here have any suggestions?'

The speech had clearly been well planned. Personally I found it a bit false. Emily was too much the well-nourished hipster, too much the aspiring Earth Mother to be altogether convincing as a religious neurotic. But there was no doubt that Robert took her case extremely seriously. After pursing his lips in thought and scratching an imaginary itch below his lip, he looked at her reassuringly and told her that her problems were not uncommon. He had known plenty of 'sensitive young people' who had been exhausted by the intensity of their studies, the loftiness of their spiritual aspirations and the ghastliness of world capitalism. The secret was not to worry too much and not to go out on extremes. There was no need for Emily to give up her partying, since the rave scene embodied a 'desire for transcendence that every sentient being needs to explore'. (In my mind's ear I can still hear Robert swallow heavily as he pronounced the word 'desire'.) On the other hand, there was certainly a need for outside intervention of some kind. Perhaps this was a case in which faith healing might be of use. 'As it happens', Robert said, 'I know a number of esoteric techniques that could probably unblock your cosmic energies. Would you like me to minister to you?'

Emily nodded her assent and Robert told her to stand up and relax. She clambered to her feet with a theatrical groan and stood there with her bare arms swinging charmingly at her side. Robert lifted himself out of the lotus position and stood directly in front of her, pressing the tips of his fingers together and looking devout. The performance was about to begin. Bending his knees and arching his back like a victim of spina bifida, Robert inhaled deeply and raised both his palms until they were parallel with Emily's face. Then he shuffled slowly and carefully all around her, keeping his hands at the same level so that the healing powers in his fingertips would irradiate her skull from every angle. Lobbo and his friend looked on in awestruck silence. Out of the corner of my eye I saw a candle flickering and a stick of incense glowing like coal. The room suddenly seemed much darker than I previously thought.

Robert performed three laps of his patient and then changed tactics. After staring unblinkingly at Emily he moved around behind her and rested his palms on the back of her head. In a matter of seconds he slid them down to her neck and shoulders, emitting a strange tubercular snort that made him sound a bit like a copulating hedgehog. By the time he reached her lower back the startling truth had become clear. In Robert's opinion – an opinion sanctified by years of meditation and spiritual sacrifice – Emily would not be cured until his healing hands had touched her from head to toe. Suddenly the tension in the room became unbearable. What in God's name would happen when those ethereal fingers moved a bit lower? Our answer came soon enough. In a moment of supreme farce, easily the equal of anything in Farquhar or Wycherley, Robert squatted uncertainly on his haunches and reached solicitously for Emily's buttocks. 'Excuse me', she responded, 'but what the *fuck* do you think you're doing?' Then she flounced off to the wall, switched on the electric light and gave Robert a ball-freezing stare before opening the door and disappearing into the street. Almost immediately I rushed to join her, scared beyond reason by the thought that I'd just witnessed a sex crime. On the way out I took the precaution of saying a prayer and stepping over the threshold four times. Just to be sure.

I got to know Emily quite well in the few weeks between her departure from the Moltmann Society and the end of the summer. We orbited different planets and there was never any chance of our colliding with each other, but from time to time we'd meet in Emma's and spend a couple of hours chatting. The flow of laughter, coffee and gossip always seemed effortless because so little was at stake. Emily took immense pleasure in teasing me about my conservatism. Aghast at my ignorance of contemporary music and my nervousness about drugs, she continually urged me to cast off the sackloth and ashes and embrace my youth. I had never known anyone who could talk so fast. Speeding through her sentences like a wayward princess channelling the spirit of Jackson Pollock, she made the previous weekend's raves sound like a bacchanalian paradise: 'The buzz was simply amazing, honey – simply *mind blowing*!' I soon realised that her libertarian instincts were more highly developed than her religious side. Her commitment to radical Christianity was sincere enough in its way but it was scarcely very fervent. What she really wanted was to be left alone to enjoy herself. The darkest villains in her youthful universe were the policemen, journalists and politicians who had tried to demonise the rave scene. Whenever she spoke about them her eyes rolled heavenwards, her arms flailed about crazily and her cheeks turned scarlet with exasperation. Her suspicion of authority was far more visceral than mine had ever been.

On a hot Saturday towards the end of August I gave in to Emily's nagging and accompanied her to a rave. It was the only one I ever attended and I look back on it as a brief interlude of pleasure in a self-destructive age. Although my compulsive illness was still putting me through hell, I sometimes had the strength to hold it at bay for a few hours at a time. That evening I experienced a sense of calm for the first time in months. I called on Emily at about eight o'clock and for a while we ambled through the city, waiting for the sky to get dark. She was due to go back to college the following week and I knew I wouldn't see her very much after that. For half an hour or so we sat on a bench on the main thoroughfare and watched the world go by. The heat had brought the punters out in their hundreds and everywhere we looked there were bronzed townies in check shirts, screeching girls tottering on high heels and older women wearing too much lipstick. The smell of beer, deodorant and urine was nothing if not pungent. Surveying the scene with an air of amused benevolence, Emily asked the question that I had been expecting all evening: 'So then, honey – Will you be taking Ecstasy tonight or not?' In spite of all my doubts I said yes straightaway. I had never taken drugs before but this was not a night for retreating into abstemiousness. My initiation into the chemical paradise was by no means steeped in ritual. After buying two bottles of water from a street vendor we walked to the beach and sat cross-legged on the sand. Emily swallowed a tablet with a quick gulp of water and then passed half a tablet to me. I popped it onto the tip of my tongue, said a quick

'Hasta la vista' to my years of narcotic innocence and washed it down before I could change my mind. For some reason I was completely free of fear. A light breeze blew soothingly across the sand and the sea did a crystalline shimmer as I waited for the Ecstasy to take effect. Emily's encouraging smile was all the reassurance I needed.

It sometimes seems as if everyone who went to a rave in the 1980s has written about his first experience of 'doing an E'. Most of these accounts are heavy with communitarian feeling, evoking the deep sense of mutual sympathy that the drug unleashed in the adolescent psyche. They ask us to believe that at the sharp end of the twentieth century, in fields, streets and dancehalls throughout the country, young Britons discovered the secret of loving their neighbours as they loved themselves. Simply to dance in a circle with Ecstasy coursing through one's veins was to feel suddenly, overwhelmingly and indissolubly united with everyone else. 'I was overcome by an unspeakably massive wave of passion that still sends a shiver down my spine', writes Olivia Gordon in *The Agony of Ecstasy*: 'I was living the existence I had always wanted.'[50]

My own experience of Ecstasy was completely different. That first tablet hit my bloodstream in fifteen minutes but my feelings for suffering humanity remained the same. I fell in love with no one and my powers of empathy failed to stir. What I did feel was an astonishing sense of serenity. Ecstasy worked on my nervous system like an industrial-strength tranquilliser, slowing me down until the distinction between sleeping and waking disappeared. For a few hours I stretched and yawned and sighed in an orgy of mindfulness. All sense of urgency had drained away. Instead of glancing feverishly from this to that and back again – instead of trying to have it all now, this instant, this second – I allowed my indolent gaze to settle on anything it liked for as long as it liked. The result was that the membrane between 'out there' and 'in here' became staggeringly permeable. The object world impinged on my senses like never before. I

50 Olivia Gordon, *The Agony of Ecstasy* (London: Continuum, 2004), p. 30.

could hardly remember a time when the sea had been wetter, the breeze so soothing or the sand between my toes so grainy. Everything seemed to pullulate in its own materiality.

The rave that night was held on the second floor of a dilapidated hotel on High Street. It was hardly the sort of numinous environment in which enlightenment is easily achieved. Apparently the hotel did most of its business renting cheerless rooms to dole claimants – some of whom were occasionally found dead in their beds after injecting rogue heroin – and no one had thought to refurbish it in many years. Even with the lights down low, coloured lasers scything through the air and dry ice rising from the floor like mist, the place still reeked of lumpenproletarian squalor. None of this mattered. By the time I got there the Ecstasy had disabled my internal censor. Emily took me by the hand as soon as we paid the entrance fee and led me giggling onto the dancefloor, where we proceeded to do our stuff until three in the morning. The music and the dancing were unlike anything I had ever encountered. Resoundingly synthetic and seemingly devoid of human input, the records reverberating from the speakers hinted at a future in which the robotic had edged out the organic. It was as if an unimaginably sophisticated computer had acquired a life of its own, composed a handful of spectral melodies and resolved to play them until humanity berserked itself into a higher dimension. One track struck me as especially compelling and I asked Emily to name the artist. She told me that she didn't know and didn't care. This was a cult in which the experience of the votaries meant more than the identity of the priests.

I had never been much of a dancer and it took me quite a while to adapt to the house style. The curious thing was that people seemed more active above the belt than below it. All night their legs trotted doggedly on the spot but their torsos and arms bristled with energy. Emily was a case in point. Looking heart-rendingly gamine (and not a little sweaty) in her flimsy black dress, she made no attempt to change her position in relation to everyone else. Instead she gyrated explosively at the hips and allowed her hands to describe weird arabesques in front of her chest. I'd secretly been hoping that dancing together would propel us towards new heights of intimacy, but I knew within twenty minutes that my vague dreams of concupiscence were doomed. The more she twisted and gesticulated – at one moment closing her eyes and at the next gazing raptly into the middle distance – the more remote she became. The same was true of everyone around us. There was simply no trace of the communal enthusiasms that Emily had led me to expect. All of us were absorbed in our own inwardness, monitoring the music with growing excitement as it zigzagged its way through our sweltering but temporarily exalted bodies. Solipsism was the order of the day. The slogan on our banner wasn't 'United we stand, divided we fall' but 'Private – please keep out!' The idea of the autonomous individual had never seemed so appealing.

The drugs had worn off by the following morning. Summer turned abruptly to autumn and the men from the council swept fallen leaves into neat piles. The last hundred days of the 1980s began their inexorable countdown. Emboldened by my experiences over the summer, I resolved to restore myself to rude good health by the time the new decade dawned. In some respects my optimism was reasonable enough. The one thing I'd learned over the previous few weeks was that tyranny should never be met with compromise. My religious delusions were as intrusive as ever, goading me every day into lengthy rituals of prayer and propitiation, but after that sudden access of blasphemy at Robert's house I knew in my bones that God's unreasonable demands could sometimes be resisted. All I needed to do was to find the right method for exorcising Him from my life forever. Hope also wafted up from other sources. After many agonising months my alienation from the life of the mind was beginning to come to an end. Once again I could open a book and expect to understand it, even if the effort required to do so was often exhausting. Naturally this inclined my thoughts in the direction of politics. Now that the fog of doctrinal confusion was lifting – now that I could once again tell my Marx from my Engels and my Lenin from my Mao – I began to think of re-establishing contact with my friends in the Party. I hadn't been active for more than a year but I knew that Linda, Bob and the others would all be pleased to see me. When I looked ahead to the person I wanted to be when the clocks chimed in the first day of 1990, I saw an energetic young man whose season of spiritual agony was at last behind him. The future was politics. The future was socialism.

Things didn't work out quite as I planned. Late in September I paid a visit to the doctor and told her about my mental problems, ruefully admitting that I knew my behaviour was ridiculous but that I couldn't seem to snap out of it. She heard me out sympathetically and mentioned a retired psychiatrist who lived nearby and still saw private patients. 'I can personally recommend him', she said. 'Would you like me to phone and make an appointment?' Two days later I drove to his large house overlooking the beach and he let me in. He turned out to be an aristocratic Pole with perfect manners and a cravat under his shirt. He began by asking me some general questions about my life and trying to put me at my ease. When he heard that I was studying for a doctorate he looked up approvingly and said 'Splendid! What's your subject?' I told him I was working on a topic in the history of Marxism and suddenly he looked so glum, so haunted by the Ghost of Oppressions Past that I almost asked him whether he wanted to talk about it. Taking off his glasses and rubbing his tired eyes, he looked at me ironically and said 'My family had to flee from Warsaw after the communists came to power'. In the end his attitude was a briskly expeditious one. He told me that my condition was 'reasonably serious' but that it didn't require therapy. The problem was that my brain chemistry was badly out of balance and needed to be put right. The only solution was to take a lengthy course of anti-depressants and wait for things to improve. Within five minutes of the diagnosis I'd written him a cheque, he'd written me a prescription and I'd driven away in search of a pharmacist. The last thing he said was 'In two or three months you should be back to normal'.

In the car on the way home I felt absolutely wonderful. The sun was shining brightly and the sky seemed as serene as an untroubled mind. Paying heartfelt thanks to industrial civilisation for the glorious gift of science, I marvelled at the thought that a handful of pills would soon make me better. By nightfall my mood had changed. Lurid incidents from the underbelly of medicine began to veer up from the unconscious. I sat at my desk and thought of all the horror stories, all the human catastrophes that doctors had inflicted on their trusting subjects. Babies rendered limbless by Thalidomide, minds befuddled by Valium, cancer patients murdered by Therac 25 – nothing escaped my jaundiced memory. How could I be sure that the doctor's orders would do me any good? Wasn't it more likely that they would simply make things worse? I knew then that my anti-depressants would remain in their packet. The vengeful God whose injunctions thundered through my brain had been cleverer than I expected. On the edge of defeat, confronted by the scientific mind in all its sceptical majesty, He had driven a wedge between my chemical saviours and me. The time for sanity was not yet.

Nor were things going well in politics. On the fifth of November – I remember the date because it was early in the evening and fireworks had begun to erupt in the sky – I bumped into Linda outside the dole office on High Street. She gave me a faint smile but I could tell immediately that she disapproved of my prolonged absence from the Party. I told her that I'd been unwell and that my illness (I didn't tell her what it was) had its roots in my desperation to acquire knowledge – a desperation ultimately sparked by my interest in Marxism. Slightly to my surprise she knew exactly what I was talking about. 'Listen, comrade', she said. 'Your experience isn't unusual. Marxism makes intense demands on people and not everyone is able to cope. Revolutionary parties expect their members to spend all their time studying, attending meetings or selling newspapers.

One of the reasons they're so small is that they've run thousands of young people into the ground. But you've got to be strong, boy. I know you've been ill but you've got to dust yourself down and get back to us as soon as you can. We'll be needing you in the struggles ahead.' Her tone was tender rather than hectoring and I appreciated the fact that she seemed to care. I touched her lightly on the arm and assured her that I'd attend the next Party meeting without fail. This seemed to satisfy her. And then – as a police siren screamed in the distance and another firework burst above our heads – she made a statement whose combination of plaintiveness, exasperation and despair will remain with me until the day I die: 'Mind you, there may not be a Party to work for if things go on as they are. It looks as if the comrades in Eastern Europe have ballsed things up nicely.'

It's not as if I'd been unaware of what was going on. I knew perfectly well that the socialist regimes in the East were beginning to look vulnerable – that the Polish communists had gone down to a humiliating defeat in free elections in June (naturally this didn't mean that they actually had to leave office) and that the Hungarians, East Germans and Bulgarians had all had their problems with the opposition. But for some reason I didn't realise how serious things were until I saw the worry in Linda's eyes. For years she'd been bullishly optimistic about the prospects of 'actually existing socialism', insisting that everything in the Stalinist garden was lovely. Now she was talking as if counter-revolution was all but inevitable. Her pessimism gave me quite a jolt. Could it be possible that the tides of History were about to go into reverse?

The endgame arrived more rapidly than any of us could have imagined. Less than forty-eight hours after my conversation with Linda, in the face of peaceful but implacably defiant protests throughout the country, East Germany's rulers decided to stand down the sentries at the Berlin Wall. The Iron Curtain had been breached! Tearful citizens poured through the checkpoints and embraced their bewildered compatriots in the West. Young people clambered onto the Wall and hacked away at it with pickaxes, holding chunks of rubble up to the cameras as if to say 'Marxism-Leninism does not a prison make'. There was no point pretending that everything would be back to normal in the morning. All across Europe the House of Marx was crashing down, demolished by the very people it was supposed to shield from harm. The workers' states were being destroyed by the workers themselves.

My immediate response to those cataclysmic events was pretty ungenerous. Not for one moment did I feel like whooping in the streets or toasting the arrival of a new era. Instead I was completely taken aback by the ease with which I accepted what was happening. To put it crudely, I knew the game was up. Watching the news in a comfortable lounge in South Wales, eating Mint Imperials from a paper bag and getting up occasionally to make a cup of tea, I realised in my gut that thousands of people in the East had suffered for forty years for precisely nothing. How obvious it seemed in retrospect that they had been heading down a cul-de-sac from day one! How stupid of them to suppose that the market could ever be bucked! All my sophisticated ideas about unleashing the potential of socialism through democratic reform – all my pious Trotskyist cant about building socialism with a human face – had been exposed for the nonsense that it was. I felt a bit like a frightened spectator at the transformation of my own soul. As communism made a hurried exit from the part of my brain marked 'cherished beliefs', the detritus of bourgeois ideology seemed to flood in to fill the vacuum. That night in Swansea, as Stalinism breathed its last, no one sensed the absurdity of Marxism more acutely than I did.

CHAPTER 7
Return of the Prodigal Comrade

My slightly histrionic response to the collapse of the Berlin Wall was shortlived. When I woke up the following morning I discovered that my Damascene conversion to world capitalism had been reversed in my sleep. So what if the long-suffering inmates of a few Stalinist hellholes had opted for the free market? Now more than ever, or so I told myself, people like me had to keep the socialist flame burning in perilous times. Our role was to hold out the vision of a genuinely creative, genuinely democratic society that one day – long after the market panaceas of the age had been exploded – might once again attract ordinary people to the socialist cause. Like a cuckolded husband whose loyalty to his wife outweighed his desire to leave her, I decided that I was in it for the long haul.

I cannot honestly say that I was driven by intellectual conviction. In my more candid moments I realised that Francis Fukuyama, the most celebrated political commentator of the day, might be right in saying that we had finally arrived at the 'end of history'.[51] Perhaps human beings would have to make do with an uninspiring combination of free markets, representative institutions and welfare states until the planet crumbled beneath us. What really kept me stuck in a Marxist groove was an overwhelming sense of exhaustion. Struggling vainly to keep my religious mania at bay – still unwilling to take my medication or seek further psychiatric help – I was simply too tired to rethink my view of the world. At an age when

51 See Francis Fukuyama, 'The End of History?', *The National Interest*, Summer 1989.

most people exult in broadening their horizons, I became as intellectually conservative as a man of seventy. Marxism was what I knew and Marxism was where I would stay.

But there was more to it than that. At some level of my mind I began to think of Marxism as a form of therapy. As I reread some of the classic texts, registering their nuances more fully than I ever had before, I realised that what really drove Marx forward was his vision of the free individual. Appalled by wage slavery and the corruption of human nature that went with it, he foresaw a time in which fully liberated men and women would take their own decisions, set their own agendas and hone their own creativity in complete independence from external authorities. Not for nothing did he and Engels describe communist society as a place where the 'free development of each is the condition for the free development of all'.[52] In the throes of self-obsession it seemed natural to take these ideas and apply them to my personal struggles. When I'd sat on the floor in Hanover Street and vowed to fight against God with every ounce of blasphemy at my disposal – or when I'd danced at the rave with Emily and experienced the siren voice of autonomy as it provoked everyone into doing their own thing – I knew in my blood that I would only get better if I had the courage to be free. What Marx seemed to tell me was that my longing for freedom was perfectly realistic. His message was that human beings were never intended to bow the knee to a vengeful God. By keeping faith with the idea of communist man I could one day make myself well.

In the end I persisted with my pale imitation of commitment for a good eighteen months after the Berlin Wall came down. The Party had never been so inactive and I suppose that suited me well. All I had to do was attend the occasional meeting, sign the occasional petition and go leafleting every two months or so. Then, one fine Monday morning in August 1991, I turned on the television in the lounge and swooned with disbelief as

52 Karl Marx and Frederick Engels, *Manifesto of the Communist Party* (Moscow: Progress Publishers, 1977), p. 60.

History threw us another dirty curve. 'Hardliners' in Moscow had staged a coup against Mikhail Gorbachev, determined to bring his programme of reforms to an end. By the end of the week the coup had collapsed and the Soviet Union effectively ceased to exist. This time I had no more commitment to give. I would not attend another Party meeting for nearly seven years.

My memories of those August days are still vivid. Even on that first morning, with John Simpson of the BBC reporting live from Moscow, it became clear that the Soviet government could no longer govern as decisively as before. Casting a disdainful eye over Gennady Yanayev and the other anti-Gorbachev plotters, Simpson described them as 'yesterday's men' who had no answers to the problems of modern Russia. Certainly they looked seedy enough, sitting there at a Kremlin news conference with their pasty complexions and their nervously tapping feet. The thought began to take hold that the coup would be resisted. Simpson and others sketched out an apocalyptic scenario in which the Soviet people took to the streets, confronted the army and demanded that Gorbachev be restored to office. Everyone feared that much blood would be spilled before the issue was settled.

For a few hours we all expected the worst. Thousands of discontented Muscovites flocked to the parliament building or 'White House', intent on defending a symbol of democracy against the diktats of an unelected elite.[53] It was clear that any battle for the future of Russia would take place there. How long could it be before the army encircled the protesters, instructed them to disperse and then opened fire when they failed to do so? By sundown nothing had happened. I stayed up all night to watch the coverage on Channel Four. In a way it was all a bit comic. A sole British camera was positioned above the entrance to a tunnel from which the Russian tanks were thought likely to emerge. Not even a stray dog put in an appearance. All we saw for minutes at a time was a quiet stretch of road and the glare

53 The Russian parliament possessed very little power but its members had been freely elected in 1990.

of a streetlight. A gallimaufry of soporific guests droned on and on in a studio in London, many of them traumatised socialists who couldn't accept that history was leaving them behind. Tony Benn assured us that the Soviet Union still possessed immense strength. Jimmy Reid, once the Communist Party's most famous member, opined that the Russian people wanted to reform socialism but not to get rid of it. By daybreak the irrelevance of what they had to say was obvious to everyone. The night had passed and not a single innocent life had been snuffed out in the name of Marxism-Leninism. The crowds outside the White House looked young, optimistic and alive with a sense of their own power. For the first time we dared to hope that the army would not be showing up.

We were almost right. An attack of sorts did occur but it ended in ignominy. As Soviet soldiers advanced on the White House in the early hours of Wednesday morning, they found themselves trapped in the same tunnel to which Channel Four had attached such significance. It turned out that the protesters had constructed an impenetrable barricade out of fridges and shopping trolleys. After that it was all over. Gorbachev flew back to Moscow after languishing under house arrest in the Crimea. His first move was to have the plotters sacked. His second was to declare that *glasnost* and *perestroika* were back on track. For a while it seemed that the *status quo ante* had been fully restored, but then came the twist in the tale that none of us had foreseen. The spoils of war went not to Gorbachev but to Boris Yeltsin, the elected Mayor of Moscow whose opposition to the coup had made all the difference. Playing his hand to perfection, Yeltsin realised that now was the time to bury the Soviet monolith forever. On Saturday he bullied Gorbachev into resigning as General Secretary of the Communist Party. A few hours later he signed the Party's death warrant by nationalising every last piece of its property. The world had well and truly been turned upside down. Shortly afterwards came the *grand guignol* announcement that no one could quite believe: The Soviet Union would cease to exist on the last day of December.

Once the coup had been defeated I spoke to a number of local communists, all of whom declared that the only thing to do was to soldier on until the bad times came to an end. Somehow I knew that none of them would still be in the Party in five years' time. All the straws we'd been clutching at had disappeared overnight. As long as the Soviet Union still existed – as long as the heirs of Lenin pretended that the workers exercised power from the sultry plains of Turkmenistan to the snowy wastes of Siberia – I'd been able to convince myself that things would one day come right. Now I had no buttress for my youthful illusions. It wasn't a case of one set of beliefs being substituted for another. I didn't slough off my Marxist skin in the morning and wrap myself in the mantle of liberalism, conservatism or social democracy in the afternoon. It was more a matter of seeing without the crutch of ideology for the first time in years. Watching the people of Moscow as they remade the city in the image of their own euphoria, I didn't need to be told that they had every right to reach for a new way of life. One incident in particular sticks in my mind – I suspect it sticks in everyone's. Late on Monday afternoon, radiating the same blend of guile and innocence that the world came to know so well, Boris Yeltsin clambered onto a tank and beseeched a crowd of protesters to resist the Soviet tyranny. The way he greeted the tank commander was astonishingly moving. Thrusting out his hand like a boisterous Georgian peasant, beaming from ear to ear as if the weight of the world were about to be lifted from his shoulders, he seemed to embody the indomitable spirit of Tolstoy's Russia at the moment of its reawakening. 'Brother', he seemed to say. 'You and I have suffered much. The motherland has been drenched in blood by those who thought they could turn it into paradise. I beg you not to help them again. Let us start afresh with love in our hearts and a lively sense of our own limitations.' The symbolism screamed across the aether. The first time I saw it on the news a line from a poem of Kenneth Rexroth's popped unbidden into my mind: ' ... one of the great things of my life had happened.'[54] Tears flowed. The indecency of siding with the bureaucracy was no longer an option.

At the beginning of December I realised with a start that the Soviet Union had little more than four weeks to live. Because my life would have been very different without it, I wanted to do something to mark its passing – something quiet, understated, not too self-indulgent. The only thing I ended up doing was reading Laurens van der Post's *Journey into Russia*, a copy of which I'd bought a few years earlier and never opened. Written in the 1960s at the point when the Khrushchev era was coming to an end, the book was a dense, evocative and self-consciously prophetic record of van der Post's epic travels across the whole of the Soviet Union. I read it as slowly as I could, lingering over the details until images of Soviet life hovered in front of my eyes like holograms. For one last time I revelled in the bizarre cast of characters that the socialist experiment had thrown up – sinister bureaucrats in shoddy suits, insanely hospitable farm workers, subversive clowns in urban circuses. The way of life that van der Post described seemed as solid as the walls of the Lubyanka Prison, but now – less than thirty years later – it was receding into history with bewildering speed. What on earth had brought everything to such an ignominious end? *Journey into Russia* provided a couple of clues. One of its arguments was that revolutionaries are so fixated by the future that they lose the capacity to appreciate the present. Watching a lugubrious delegation of communists at a hotel on the Black Sea coast, van der Post was so taken aback by their lack of 'joy' that he ventured an iron law of political life: 'The quintessence of it [i.e. the revolutionary movement] is perhaps that the original love of life, of justice and of man which gave birth to Communism has long since been cast out and forgotten.'[55] There was also the issue of geography. On a flight from Moscow to Tashkent, van der Post spoke to an Armenian Colonel who told him that

54 Kenneth Rexroth, 'GIC to HAR' in *The Collected Shorter Poems of Kenneth Rexroth* (New York: New Directions, 1968), p. 108.

55 Laurens van der Post, *Journey into Russia* (Harmondsworth: Penguin Books, 1976 [1964]), p. 146.

Russia's vast size – the sheer bewildering diversity of its terrain – had marked the national character forever. The experience of being surrounded by endless acres of land, much of it wild and uncultivated, imbued nearly everyone in the country with a permanent sense of melancholy:

> This Russian now told me that it was right to begin with a feeling of the immensity of the land. I must build on that as perhaps the greatest single fact necessary for understanding his people and his native country. But he feared that it would take time before a stranger could realize how immense the land was. He wished he could convey all that immensity to me not just as a physical fact but also as the emotion that was in him and all his countrymen.[56]

The idea that geography determines human nature was already familiar to me. I knew about Bloch, Braudel and all those other historians from *Annales* who attached the highest significance to mountains, coastlines and the quality of the land. Yet there was something about van der Post's prose that depressed me enormously. Ever since reading Marx I'd assumed that human beings are moulded by things that can ultimately be changed – states, ideologies, modes of production. The thought that Russians were condemned to being Russians by the vastness of their territory struck me as slightly obscene. As disillusioned as I was, I swore that intellectual pessimism of that sort would never take possession of my soul. Perhaps my long journey back to Marxism began there.

On New Year's Eve I went to the pub with some friends. None of them seemed aware that one of history's greatest reversals was about to occur – or perhaps they knew perfectly well and didn't want to rub my nose in it. As midnight approached, unable to resist the lure of melodrama, I went outside on my own and listened to the distant sound of the sea. When midnight struck I imagined the red flag being lowered above the Kremlin for the

56 Ibid., p. 63.

last time. Suddenly the world seemed emptier, less interesting. I raised my glass to the inky black sky and drank a silent toast to all the men and women who had tried and failed to liberate mankind. Then, embarrassed by my sentimentality, I drank another toast to all the men and women whom the Soviet Union had done to death. There was nothing left to do but to go back inside and order another vodka.

In the years that stretched ahead I spent most of my time in ideological limbo. On the face of it I adapted well to a world in which revolutionary hopes were regarded as perverse. I began to describe myself as a libertarian of the soft-left who wanted a bit more money for the poor, a bit more power for the trade unions and a bit more freedom for the individual. The only problem was that memories of life before the fall were always intruding. I began to realise that no one who really immerses himself in Marxism can ever entirely leave it behind. Even if a man retires to the countryside, writes learned tomes on market economics or becomes an activist in the Conservative Party, he will always be beleaguered by an agonising sense of what life had once been like. The contrast between the dour moderation of today and the invigorating extremism of yesterday will tear him apart. At the dead of night, transfixed by the utopian arias that flow up through the cracks in his internal censor, he will dare to ask himself whether the intensities of his youth might still be recaptured. Can all the old heresies be resurrected? Can the spirit still quicken at the thought of industrial struggle, working-class advance and the transition to socialism? Most people respond to these questions by pretending that they never asked them. My burden was that I could never quite get them out of my mind. Like a lapsed Catholic who finds himself in the vicinity of a church whenever a service is about to begin, I found myself drawn by an irresistible force to the old texts, the old meeting halls, the old loyalties. At first I thought that my inability to flush out the Marxist virus was purely a symptom of psychological transition, a sort of necessary confrontation with the past that would eventually allow me to move on to better things. In fact the opposite was the case. The more I thought about Marxism – the longer I allowed its categories to shape my thinking even as I tried to resist them – the more I became convinced that life without it would be meaningless. After a while the bewildering truth was borne in upon me: I was not bidding adieu to Marxism but preparing to embrace it at a higher level of understanding. I was making my way down the road to Damascus for the second time.

The long march from disillusionment back to commitment was never straightforward. Along the way there were all sorts of deviations, reversals and crises. The first sign that something strange was happening was that my mind began playing tricks on me. From time to time, usually at moments of extreme tiredness or melancholy, I got the distinct impression that the past had burst its boundaries and was flooding into the present. It was as if the events of the last few years had never occurred and the old world still existed. Like a poor man's Proust I'd be possessed by memories of what belonging to the socialist movement had actually *felt like.* Images of interminable Party meetings in poorly lit rooms, impassioned demonstrations on windy city streets and snatched conversations in radical bookshops invaded my mind for long stretches of time, blotting out mundane reality and stopping my ears to the tedious music of the present. Sometimes these experiences were not merely disorienting but positively vertiginous. On one occasion, leafing through a copy of György Lukács's *Studies in European Realism* in the university library, I was catapulted back about ten years to the afternoon when I'd first taken the book off the shelves. Suddenly I was sixteen again and Lukács's Hungary was still socialist, Arthur Scargill still bestrode the land like a militant colossus and Marxism was still the wave of the future. The sense of disjuncture was so overwhelming that for a few moments I actually felt dizzy. Steadying myself on one of the shelves in front of me, I cursed the passage of time and everything it had done to the world and me.

I wasn't the only person in post-communist Europe for whom these strange time lapses became a part of everyday life. In the years since I've come across plenty of people who experienced something similar. My favourite anecdote about the socialist past melting into the capitalist present can be found in Wolf Biermann's great essay 'Shaking Hands with the Zeitgeist', which I first read a few years after its publication in 1992. The essay records what happened when Biermann, a writer and musician who had been expelled from East Germany in the 1970s, met Mikhail Gorbachev in a reception in Hamburg shortly after the collapse of the Soviet Union. Although Biermann had not called himself a Marxist in many years, he found that merely being in the same room as a former Soviet leader induced an overpowering wave of nostalgia. When the two men shook hands, the only thing Biermann could think to say was 'I am a Communist.'[57] What was extraordinary was that Gorbachev responded in kind. Caught off guard in the heartlands of the capitalist West, the man who had done more than anyone else to destroy international socialism palpably seemed to brighten. The old ideological reflexes came surging back and an electric current of revolutionary enthusiasm convulsed his stocky frame. For a few seconds the two men were trapped in a historical bubble, oblivious to the publishing executives and journalists who swarmed around them. Then Gorbachev broke the spell: ' … he squeezed meaningfully and tragically, communicating what we both knew very well: it doesn't matter any more.'[58] To this day I can hardly read Biermann's final paragraph without feeling cut to the quick by the intensity of its regret:

> At the moment of our handshake Gorbachev stiffened meaningfully. We were silent for a brief eternity. I even had the feeling that the habit of this rite of fraternal affection practised thousands upon thousands of times would propel

57 Wolf Biermann, 'Shaking Hands with the Zeitgeist', translated by Martin Chalmers, *Granta*, No. 42, Winter 1992, p. 156.

58 Ibid., p. 159.

> Gorbachev into giving me a fraternal kiss ... Fortunately this chalice passed me by. So we stood there, two survivors by the open grave of a fixed idea. Then we went on our way.[59]

The point of Biermann's essay was that his remembrance of times past finally cured him of any residual commitment to socialism. As bittersweet as the momentary resurrection of his younger self had been, it prompted him to think long and hard about Stalinism's exorbitant crimes. After that the light from his socialist youth had been snuffed out forever. My own response to the reverberations of the past was very different. In my more abstract moments I became preoccupied with the nature of historical memory, sensing that the flow of time can only be made bearable if we recognise that the past continues to exist so long as people are still around to recall it.[60] But more than anything else I stopped thinking about socialism in such floridly elegiac terms. The temptation after 1991 had been to regard international communism as a failure on a truly catastrophic scale. The consensus among former believers was that Lenin and his heirs were well-meaning bunglers who achieved precisely nothing. Now, in the grip of memories too vivid to be dismissed out of hand, I began to feel my way towards a more nuanced position. Not yet daring to hope that Marxism might have a future, I tried to draw up a balance sheet of its past. The crimes of communism were unforgivable – nothing could persuade me otherwise. But surely the movement I'd belonged to for nearly a decade had *some* achievements to its credit? As I strove to answer that question, I took to arguing that Marxists had been more successful with means than with ends. Their failure to establish socialism was more or less total but along the way they did us all a few favours. At first my perspective

59 Ibid., p. 161.

60 My primitive musings on this theme eventually led me to the work of the great Marxist critic John Berger, whose scepticism towards linear theories of time is an integral part of his writings on contemporary culture. See, inter alia, John Berger, 'Painting and Time' in *The White Bird* (London: The Hogarth Press, 1988 [1985]), pp. 205-211.

was a pretty solipsistic one. Because the communist movement had educated me more effectively than any number of schools, colleges and universities, I rhapsodised about its extraordinary success in raising the cultural level of ordinary people. A bit later, inspired by the wave of scholarship that poured out of Western universities as the Soviet archives were opened up to historians, I started to think in much broader terms. I owed a particular debt to Eric Hobsbawm, whose titanic *Age of Extremes* (1994) balanced a world-weary awareness of the Soviet Union's failings against a cussed insistence that its influence had sometimes been beneficent. Hobsbawm's implied argument was that the Soviet government had done more for the world at large than for its own people. Unfailingly inefficient and frequently draconian at home, it had a sterling record of provoking capitalist governments into establishing welfare states and making concessions to the workers' movement. Its role in the defeat of fascism was heroic and its support for liberation movements in the Third World did much to rid the world of empires. These were achievements that anyone could be proud of.[61]

The problem with all this careful retrospection was that it was better suited to old age than to what Leszek Kolakowski once called 'dream-hungry youth'. Hobsbawm was nearly eighty when *Age of Extremes* came out and most of his passion had been spent. It was probably quite easy for the world's most distinguished historian to sit wearily in his study, acknowledge that the cause to which he devoted his life had failed and derive some small crumbs of comfort from its incidental achievements. Those of us who were fifty years younger found it less easy to lay the spectre of political commitment to rest. Having persuaded ourselves that the first wave of workers' states had done some good, it was only a matter of time until we dared to hope that socialism's moment might one day come again. In many respects our outlook was that of spoilt children. Our desires drove us forward even though the real world seemed to tell us

61 See Eric Hobsbawm, *Age of Extremes: The Short Twentieth Century 1914-1991* (London: Michael Joseph, 1995 [1994]).

that they could never be realised. In the absence of any hard evidence that socialism could work better than capitalism – in the middle of one of the longest periods of market triumphalism in history – we suppressed our doubts and noisily reaffirmed our revolutionary credentials because a world without hope was too awful to bear. Anyone who claims to have cleaved to Marxism in the 1990s solely out of intellectual conviction is probably a liar. The simple truth is that those of us who stuck with the cause were often motivated by little more than blind faith.

What it boiled down to was this: In spite of my careful Hobsbawmian musings about the past, in spite of my scrupulous liberal objections to the failures of actually existing socialism, I began to feel an overwhelming and utterly irrational desire to say 'I still believe'. At about this time I developed a strange preoccupation with a character in fiction, one whose fate I melodramatically came to associate with my own. *Professore* was the main protagonist in George Steiner's novella *Proofs* (1991), a heartbreakingly desolate and magnificently affirmative meditation on the collapse of international communism. Clearly based on the Italian philologist Sebastiano Timpanaro, author of the idiosyncratic Marxist classic *On Materialism* (1970), *Professore* lives in Rome and enjoys a hard-won reputation as the most punctilious proofreader in the city. A self-taught Marxist militant in his sixties, ascetic in his personal habits but possessed of a messianic faith in the human capacity for greatness, he finds his health collapsing at the very moment that his political universe is thrown into crisis. As the anti-communist revolt in Eastern Europe gathers pace – the novella is set in the closing months of 1989 – he struggles to come to terms with the fact that his eyesight is beginning to fail. An ophthalmologist diagnoses inoperable cataracts and advises him to change his job. He has proofread texts for nearly forty years but now his eyes are 'going on strike'.[62]

Steiner's point was not hard to fathom. *Professore* is a symbol

62 George Steiner, *Proofs and Three Parables* (London: Faber and Faber, 1992), p. 53. *Proofs* first appeared in *Granta* in 1991.

of the utopian imagination – an obsessive corrector of the printed page whose role is to 'tak[e] the errata out of history'.[63] The conjunction of personal illness and political catastrophe is no mere coincidence. By losing his sight as the masses turn their backs on socialism, *Professore* reminds us that the disappearance of the Stalinist regimes is at one and the same time a terrible crisis for human culture. Marxism has done more than anything else to keep the flames of utopia burning in a dispiriting age, or so Steiner seemed to argue. Its terminal crisis creates the awful possibility that the very idea of the good society is soon to be consigned to history. Nothing could be more dreadful. Nothing could degrade humanity more. Without utopia we are ships adrift in an endless sea.

Although Steiner wasn't a Marxist himself, the closing pages of *Proofs* fought an astonishing rearguard action against the peddlers of political despair. When I look back I realise that they went a long way towards crystallising my sense of how my own life might proceed. In the final scene, appalled by the detritus of consumer culture that seems everywhere to surround him, *Professore* musters his last resources of hope and rejoins the Italian Communist Party. There is no sound political reason for doing so. The Party is haemorrhaging members every minute and is preparing to abolish itself. *Professore*'s only motivation is his deep, urgent and magnificently untameable belief that men and women cannot be allowed to abandon their worthier selves. It is better to place a wager on an unlikely future than surrender to the grim realism of the present. No scene in fiction has ever affected me so deeply, except for one which precedes it by about fifty pages. Walking in the hills above Rome on a still October morning, *Professore* and his friend Maura discover a small column buried in the undergrowth. They soon identify it as the remnants of a Christian grave from the third or fourth century. Its inscription reads *Manet Amor*. Steiner helpfully provides a translation for those of us who lack Latin: *Manet Amor* means

63 Ibid., p. 51.

'love endures'.[64] In the context it could equally mean 'utopia persists'. Writing like this is capable of changing lives.

My fascination with the themes of memory, history and utopia was all very well in its way, but in itself it wasn't enough to bring me back to Marxism. The thing that really made politics seem relevant again was the traumatic experience of getting off my backside and finding a job. In the early 1990s I became a part-time lecturer in Higher Education, pitching my tent in a number of Welsh universities, colleges and institutes. For the first time I knew what it meant to be an oppressed worker. Employed for ludicrously short periods on fantastically exploitative contracts – sometimes going without pay for months at a time while smooth-talking Heads of Department ironed out 'local difficulties' – I did the equivalent of a full-time job for the most exiguous salary imaginable. By and large I didn't mind too much about that. What really dismayed me was the astonishingly unscrupulous behaviour of a small *fronde* of colleagues, all of whom claimed to be principled left-wingers with a passion for teaching. In those early months and years, striving to learn my craft in an environment where backstabbing counted for more than scholarship, I lost count of the number of occasions on which enthusiastic students were shortchanged, cast adrift or downright bullied by the bloodless careerists who taught them. Nearly every week brought fresh evidence of vulnerable youngsters being royally shat on by people who called themselves socialists, feminists, anti-racists or gay activists. The curious thing was that my colleagues' misdemeanours, some of which bordered on outright illegality, only rekindled my desire to return to the left. For more than ten years I'd been part of a movement that valued intellectual integrity more than anything else. The prospect of abandoning the beautiful idea of human liberation to a handful of charlatans, egotists and bigots seemed like a betrayal. How could I live with myself if I made no contribution to reclaiming the left from those who used radical

64 Ibid., p. 24.

ideology as a cover for the will-to-power? In the end it was all very simple: I returned to the fold because so many of the people inside it were rotten to the core.

There were two people in particular who embodied the higher callousness in its most heartless form. One was a dour Scotsman called Willie who served as 'subject leader' in Cultural History in the first institution I taught at. Bearded, unsmiling and prissy, Willie had been radicalised by the student rebellions of 1968 and became a communist shortly afterwards. History remembers the so-called 'Sixty-Eighters' as an irrepressible collocation of firebrands, clowns and sages. To spend ten minutes in Willie's company was to learn that history can sometimes be wrong. The man was a sort of walking incarnation of a gloomy Catholic Sunday. The joke in the department was that a bunch of daffodils had turned black and died when he bought them for a colleague as a retirement present. Even his appearance was a calculated insult to the people he was supposed to teach. Although he was traditional enough to wear a suit to work – and in that sense could be sharply distinguished from his Sixties contemporaries with their jeans and sweaters – his clothes were always crumpled, unironed, stained and musty. His ludicrous kipper ties were worn loose at the neck in a daring display of contempt for bourgeois respectability. All his colleagues had learned the art of shutting their nostrils against his appallingly noisome breath.

Willie's technique for humiliating his students evinced a certain amount of finesse. He specialised in lulling them into a false sense of security before slashing away at the jugular. At first he came across as the soul of pedagogical liberalism. As a matter of principle he never drew up a syllabus without inviting student representatives to his office to discuss their 'concerns and perspectives'. The fact that none of these discussions had the slightest impact on what the students were eventually taught was hardly the point. The important thing was that Willie had put his passionate commitment to equality on full display. He would rather have died than give a lecture in the traditional style. In the classroom he spoke for five or ten minutes and then divided the students into small groups, instructing them to discuss the 'relevance' of the week's topic to their 'own experience'. Nothing pleased him more than listening to a young girl explore the parallels between *Romeo and Juliet* and her own romantic agonies. He considered it the height of bad manners to interrupt anyone or comment critically on what they said. The only thing that ever upset him was if a student failed to address him by his Christian name. The enemies of a decent education were hierarchy, 'passive learning' and formality.

Or so it seemed. The students' impression of Willie always changed dramatically on the day he gave them their essays back. Assuming that their written work would be assessed as leniently as their contributions in class, most of them tossed off their eight sides of A4 at the last minute and with little regard for logic, structure or grammar. The response was invariably withering. Willie wielded his red pen like a scimitar, covering nearly everyone's efforts with a barrage of perpendicular lines and brutally personal comments. I once saw a paragraph of fewer than a hundred words annotated with the following examples of constructive criticism: 'Sexist rubbish', 'Adolescent pap', 'Barely literate'. The reactions to all this savagery tended to bifurcate along lines of gender. The boys stalked noisily through the corridors with the colour rising in their cheeks, swearing that Willie would be hanging from the ceiling fan in his office by the end of the day. The girls retreated to the toilets and wept until their eyes were as red as uncooked meat. Disillusionment stalked the land.

At first I thought that Willie's behaviour was simply an expression of his curiously inhuman character, not a symptom of his political beliefs. Then something happened that changed my mind. One afternoon a student flagged me down in the corridor, explained that Willie had given her an outrageously low mark and asked me to accompany her to his office so that she could 'have it out with him.' If I'd been wise I'd have told her that I couldn't be a party to a direct challenge to a colleague's competence. Instead I agreed to help her out, motivated at least in part by a slightly pathetic (and no doubt obscurely sexual) desire to be seen as the tribune of the masses. It was a swelteringly hot day and the atmosphere in Willie's office was fetid. The whole place reeked of sweat. Nervously scratching the side of her elegant alabaster neck with fingernails painted deep red – sometimes speaking clearly, at other times tripping girlishly over her words – the student aired her grievances and asked that her mark be reconsidered. Willie's wholly uncompromising response was ventilated by an air of sweet reasonableness. He explained at some length that although he 'took no pleasure' in upsetting his students, his first duty was to uphold high scholarly standards. It was no good pretending that students had done acceptable work when what they really needed was a plain-speaking exposure of their weaknesses. How else could they be expected to do better in the future?

As the torrent of self-justification continued, I fixed my gaze on two newspaper clippings that Willie had sellotaped to the edge of one of his bookshelves. The first was taken from the *Morning Star* and reported on the latest reading trends in the former USSR. Apparently the most popular authors in Russian libraries were no longer Tolstoy, Pushkin and Dostoevsky but Stephen King and Jackie Collins. The second was from the *Guardian* and relayed the melancholy fact that Russian viewers had developed an unhealthy obsession with a Mexican soap opera called *The Rich Also Cry.*[65] The juxtaposition of the two clippings brought everything home to me: *Willie was persecuting his students because the masses had let him down.* When he castigated them for their shoddy grammar or their inability to use footnotes properly, he was symbolically avenging himself on all the ungrateful wretches who had been offered literacy, culture and workers' power and opted instead for the glossy consolations of commercial TV. His insouciance in class wasn't

65 I later learned that a dying Muscovite had been so enamoured of *The Rich Also Cry* that he offered his life-savings in return for any information about how the series would end. See Joseph Pearce, *Solzhenitsyn: A Soul in Exile* (London: Harper Collins, 2000), p. 286.

a sign of academic indifference but a test of his students' mettle. By giving them the impression that little effort was required to pass his course, he was challenging them to defy his low expectations and behave like scholars in the making. When they failed to do so the full weight of his political frustrations was unleashed: He was punishing the new generation for the sins of their proletarian forebears. How could I explain all this to a visibly deflated student whose confidence had been destroyed? The simple answer was that I couldn't. The only thing I said to her after Willie sent us on our way was 'Try not to worry. He's not passing judgement on you – he's passing judgement on History itself.'

I'll say one thing for Willie: He didn't seem to mind that I'd helped a student complain about his marking. Our relationship had never exactly been effusive but it didn't get any worse after that trip to his office. It was only a few years later that standing up to the academic left actually lost me my job. At this point I had better issue an ideological health warning. It is difficult to tell this story without sounding conceited, chauvinistic or just plain mendacious, and I realise that my chief antagonist would remember things differently. But what of it? The person I'm about to introduce – my second example of academic leftism in all its bovine semi-fascist squalor – was so low, so utterly devoid of self-knowledge or common decency, that the mere act of reading about her can only make you feel good about yourself. Prepare to meet a monster.

For a few years in the Nineties I taught Cultural Studies in a Faculty of Art and Design. The name and location of the university had better be a secret. It was the only time in what passes for my career when my colleagues envied me. I was young, conscientious and personable and somehow or other my lectures regularly caught fire.[66] I was the students' favourite and everyone knew it. This state of affairs was especially disagreeable to a very ignorant art historian called Louise (or Lou for short),

66 They had never done so before and they have never done so since. I suppose it was just my time.

who – as misfortune would have it – had recently been put in charge of those of us employed on short-term contracts. It became increasingly common for students to take me to one side and tell me that Lou had made some slanderous remark about me behind my back. Some of them warned me that her jealousy was now so incendiary that sooner or later she would find an excuse for not renewing my contract. In my naiveté I assumed that not even a radical academic would seek to deprive me of my living.

Lou set a trap for me and I walked straight into it. One evening in March, during the fortnight when exam boards were being held to finalise undergraduate results for the first semester, she rang me up at about ten o' clock with a hint of wildness in her voice. She told me that she'd been looking through the marksheet for my course on cultural theory and wanted to offer me some advice. By and large the marks were fine but she thought that one essay – a solid but unspectacular effort by a quiet student called Sophie Griffiths – needed to have at least twenty marks taken off it. I asked her what was wrong with the essay and she told me that she hadn't actually read it: 'The point I'm trying to make is that Griffiths is a lazy cow who needs to be taught a lesson.' Too shocked (and perhaps too cowardly) to challenge her outright, I told her that I couldn't agree to reduce the mark but that I'd keep an eye on Sophie to make sure she was working hard enough. Things had become fairly glacial by the time the conversation ended.

The following afternoon, Sophie turned up at my office. Her pretty, delicate and expressive face seemed even paler and more bewildered than usual. I asked her what was wrong. She told me that Lou had sashayed into the student coffee bar, marched her outside and demanded that she hand over the essay from my course. Sophie had played for time by telling her that she didn't have the essay to hand and Lou had given her twenty-four hours to produce it, insisting that a vital issue of academic standards was at stake: 'I don't believe that Philip has marked your essay objectively and I want to check it out for myself.' I remember thinking that this was how wars start. Events beyond my control were forcing me to mobilise my troops and march them off to certain death in the Dardanelles. Anxious to steer Sophie away from the emotional window ledge on which she seemed to be perched, I told her that she was under no obligation to show the essay to anyone else and that I would sort things out with Lou.

'Please be careful', she pleaded. 'Lou's in a terrible temper and I think she's got it in for me.'

'Have you any idea why?'

'Yes. Not so long ago she asked me out for dinner and when I told her I couldn't go she became very hostile.'

At this point it's necessary to provide some context. I'll try to be as seemly as I can, not least because I want to make it clear that my problem wasn't with Lou's sexuality but with the way she used it to harass her students. Lou was in her mid-forties when all this was going on and had been teaching in the faculty for ten years. Born to a working-class family for whom intellectual curiosity was a sign of weakness, she had come out as a lesbian in her mid-twenties and done a degree as a mature student. She once told me that her studies in Art History had been a form of therapy for the brutal homophobia she'd experienced in her youth. Analysing the work of Frida Kahlo, Cindy Sherman or Jenny Holzer had helped her come to terms with her pain. After getting her MA she set herself up as a radical academic of the most monomaniacal kind, intruding the tenets of Lesbian Feminism into every lecture, every seminar, every snatched conversation. There was only one problem. The gulf between the undoubted worthiness of her cause and the ghastliness of her personality grew wider with every passing day. Short, palpably malign and known to students as the 'Poison Dwarf', Lou had long since transmuted her personal suffering into an overwhelming sense of entitlement. She was notorious on the gay scene for making exorbitant demands on attractive women and exposing them to furious vendettas when they failed to meet them. Sophie wasn't the first student to fall victim to her black rages – several others had learned what happens when lust curdles into hatred. No one in the Department felt able to stand up to her for fear of being labelled a bigot.

The final conflict was over and done with in a matter of minutes. In a fit of self-righteousness, fortified by what smelled like a shot of gin, Lou summoned me to an empty seminar room and asked me to explain why I'd told Sophie not to give her the essay. Even at that point I contemplated smoothing things over with an affable grin and a polite semi-apology, but when I stared into Lou's horribly corrupted face – coarse, blubberous, hungry for obedience – I suddenly felt an irresistible desire to humiliate her. For a few exhilarating moments I spoke to her as if she were a murderer or a paedophile, accusing her in a torrent of sarcasm of being a self-obsessed erotomane, a sadistic bully and a blunderingly incompetent scholar. Her response was everything I could have hoped for. Turning puce with inarticulate rage, spraying saliva in all directions as she tried and failed to bark out a reply, she slammed a fist into the desk in front of her and stormed out into the corridor. Telling truth to power felt good.

It also cost me my job. He who lives by short-term contracts eventually dies by them. Knowing that she couldn't sack me for anything – aware that my stock was too high among students and external examiners alike – Lou simply let the academic year wind down and declined to renew my contract at the start of the new term. The way she went about it spoke volumes about her character. I had worked in the Department for five years but there was no phonecall or letter to tell me that my services were no longer required. The deafening silence told me everything I needed to know. I later heard on the grapevine that Lou justified getting rid of me by telling colleagues that I had been sleeping with Sophie Griffiths. Her combination of cowardice and dishonesty was, in its way, exquisite.

I had often expressed my admiration for people who changed their lives for the better after becoming unemployed. Now I found myself having to do the same. The first thing I decided was that I would eschew the path of militancy. I could certainly have got my job back if I'd gone to the lecturers' union and made an unholy fuss, but the prospect of returning to the scene of Lou's crime seemed anything but appetising. Instead I channelled my anger into a clean break that was actually a return to earlier ambitions. Within a month of receiving my P45 I signed on at the local university to do a PhD, determined that this time I wouldn't leave my thesis unfinished. Even after so many years it seemed natural to choose a topic on the history of British Communism, in spite of the fact that I hadn't been active in the movement for nearly a decade. When my supervisor asked me at our first meeting whether I belonged to the Party, I heard myself say 'Yes – for my sins'. The following day I filled out a form in the *Morning Star* and applied to rejoin.

It wasn't simply anger at losing my job that pushed me back towards the Party. It was more the sense that Lou's behaviour exemplified everything that had gone wrong with the left since the collapse of socialism. As a noisy propagandist for Lesbian Feminism, Lou typified the less salubrious side of what some people called the 'new social movements' – the network of organisations and campaigns that fought for a fair deal for women, people of colour, sexual minorities and other oppressed groups. Although I supported all these movements, I had always been puzzled by the strain of authoritarianism that afflicted some of their members. It seemed to me that a lot of people who called themselves feminists, anti-racists or gay liberationists were often capable of gross censoriousness, taking steps to suppress views other than their own whenever they could. In a curious way it was the brouhaha with Lou which allowed me to understand what was going on. Thinking back over her serial bullying of female students, I came to regard her lack of professionalism as a symptom of the left's estrangement from universal values. The point about socialism was that it claimed to benefit *everyone.* The new social movements were altogether less messianic, insisting only that they represented the interests of particular oppressed groups. Their appeal was to women or people of colour or gays and lesbians but never to humanity as a whole.

Yet the distinction between 'universalists' and 'particularists' (to use the clotted jargon of the time) was never quite as rigid as it appeared. As Lou slammed the departmental door in my face, I was forced to recognise that the hunger for universal values lived on in the new social movements in unacknowledged form. Ostensibly, Lou only wanted to improve things for people like herself. In practice she wanted to impose her own lifestyle on people for whom it was not appropriate. When she victimised heterosexual students who refused to go out with her – when she asked girls like Sophie out to dinner and stripped them of marks when they declined – she was implicitly expressing her yearning for a politics that would be relevant to the whole of humanity. Her ferocity wasn't the symptom of a diseased personality but of her oblique, shamefaced and perhaps only semi-conscious recognition that she wanted to speak for men and women everywhere but ultimately spoke only for herself. There was nothing intrinsically intolerant about the new social movements. The problems only arose when feminists, anti-racists and gay activists feared that they had nothing to offer the rest of us. As on so many other occasions over the years, I concluded that the only solution lay in socialism. If people like Lou hitched their trailers to the Marxist wagon – if they fused their interest in gender, race and sexuality with a broader campaign for the liberation of everyone – they could satisfy their desire for universality without compromising the interests of their particular constituencies. It was necessary to revive socialism in order to save the rest of the left from its own dark temptations. That at least was what I told myself as I inspected the ruins of my career and tried to prevent my bitterness from consuming me.

There was one other matter that had to be resolved before my return to the Good Old Cause could be meaningful. The illness I had surrendered to nearly a decade earlier showed no signs of abating. Over the years I had grown used to the symptoms but their grip on my mind was as tenacious as ever. Every waking moment was defined by a frenzied *pas de deux* between obsession and compulsion. Even at the best of times I was barely functional. The real problem was that I was still too stubborn to take the necessary medication. Whenever I visited the doctor in search of a miracle cure, he wearily explained that my brain chemistry was so 'scrambled' that only a strong dose of anti-depressants held out any hope. 'You must forget this nonsense about therapy or a vigorous exercise regimen', he once said. 'Your choice is a very simple one: Either you go on Prozac or you carry on being a nutter.' His rhetoric fell on deaf ears. Convinced that the pharmaceutical industry was a vast conspiracy against the people's health, I continued to believe that some day soon I would simply wake up and will the illness to disappear.

And then, out of the blue, I was set on the road to recovery. One evening in September I had a phonecall from Julian, who told me that he would be passing through Swansea the following week and that we should meet up for a chat. I had scarcely seen him over the previous few years but from time to time I received a letter or a postcard in which he breathlessly recounted the latest stage in his ideological evolution. His days as a Marxist were long since behind him. Mildly ashamed by his involvement in the Squaddists and bewildered by the collapse of socialism in Eastern Europe, he had attached himself to a group of New Age Travellers and reinvented himself as a bearded, mantra-chanting exponent of spiritual enlightenment. These days he spent most of his time touring the country in a caravan, pitching up at raves and festivals and eking out a living by selling dope. Somehow I knew that his influence on me had not yet been exhausted. I could hardly wait to see him.

We met in a pub in the Uplands and made a pretty unlikely pair. I was still very much the overgrown schoolboy with my side parting, beige chinos and corduroy jacket. By contrast, Julian had dreadlocks down to his shoulders and wore a camouflage jacket and mud-encrusted jeans. It seemed a piquant coincidence that Paula Abdul's 'Opposites Attract' was playing on the jukebox as we shook hands and ordered the first round of drinks. Soon enough we were roaming around Swansea like the pair of perfervid teenage comrades we had once been, excitedly swapping anecdotes as we skipped lightly along the road to utopia. In the end we fetched up in Singleton Park and sat on a bench as the lights from the bay glittered in the distance. In a way it was the last enchanted evening of my adolescence, though more than ten years had gone by since I had bidden farewell to my teens. Sparking up a joint and expertly blowing smoke rings into the night air, Julian gripped my attention as he outlined his new way of looking at things. He told me that he no longer believed in the primacy of economics. After studying the work of Terence McKenna, a rather sinister American anthropologist who had become the éminence *grise* of the rave generation, he had come to the conclusion that societies are primarily shaped by their favourite recreational drug.[67] A nation which nurtures its contemplative faculties with Peyote or Hashish will live very differently to one which embraces oblivion on booze. A culture weaned on LSD is unlikely to have much in common with a culture weaned on amphetamine sulphate. The whole theory came freighted with a note of utopian promise. The historical function of Ecstasy was to usher in the earthly paradise, or so Julian assured me. Once the majority of people took the drug everyday – once every businessman and factory worker and single mother reached for a tab as automatically as they now reached for a drink – it was only a matter of time until society would be remade in the image of peace, plenty and comradeship. Marx had been wrong. It was not the working class who would save us from ourselves. The future belonged to those 'blessed alchemists' who knew the formula for methylinedioxy-methamphetamine.

I thought Julian was talking nonsense and I told him so. He gave me a tolerant smirk, as if to say 'These truths will become real to you once your mind is ready for them.' Under the force

67 McKenna outlined this theory in *Food of the Gods: The Search for the Original Tree of Knowledge* (New York: Bantam Books, 1994 [1992]). For a sceptical but witty and informative survey of McKenna's ideas, see Will Self, 'Mushrooms Galore' in *Junk Mail* (London: Penguin, 1996).

of his gaze I sensed the beginnings of an intellectual shift. I knew perfectly well that Ecstasy wasn't the great liberator we'd all been waiting for, but Julian's belief that the brain could be transformed for the better by a small white pill – that neurology and pharmacology could work magically in tandem to rid suffering humanity of its burdens – filled me with excitement. Suddenly my suspicion of the pharmaceutical industry struck me as naive and provincial. As always happened when Julian and I got together for one of our little chats, the world seem to hum with new possibilities. On the spur of the moment, determined that this time my anxieties wouldn't get the better of me, I resolved to get up early in the morning and make another appointment to see the doctor. The time for Prozac had arrived.

As the doctor wrote out my prescription he wished me luck and told me that the drugs would start to take effect in about a fortnight. Ten days later the whole ecology of my mind began to change. The horrible tension I had lived with for ten years started to ease. Sometimes I could go for five minutes at a time without being assailed by intrusive thoughts. My prayers became less frequent and less fervent. Then one morning, three or four weeks after washing down my first tablet, I woke up early to find a shaft of white light slanting across the head of the bed. It was the middle of October but the air was so pure it could have been high summer. Propping myself up on my elbow, I closed my eyes and repeated the same phrase three times: 'Now you will be better. Now you will be better. Now you will be better.' In a moment of catharsis the residues of my illness seemed to drain away like pus from a freshly lanced boil. When I opened my eyes the world had been transformed beyond all recognition. I was cured.

The Swansea Branch of the Communist Party was a much enfeebled thing by the time I rejoined it, six months or so after Tony Blair's New Labour won a landslide victory in the General Election of 1997.[68] Even at the darkest hour of the long

68 A brief history lesson is in order here. The Communist Party of Great

Thatcherite night there had been 200 people on the books, only a fraction of whom bothered to turn up to meetings. Now the entire Branch could fit quite comfortably into the Secretary's less than capacious front room. There were precisely five of us. The two oldest members were Linda (now in her sixties but still astonishingly vigorous) and an intelligent but dogmatic septuagenarian called Don who still regarded Stalin as humanity's most farsighted leader. The Branch Secretary and his French wife were considerably more youthful and not at all prone to defending the indefensible, but even so I was the youngest by a good fifteen years. It was widely said at the time that only the ageing, the deluded and the terminally nostalgic still thought communism had anything going for it. A quick glance at the Swansea Branch seemed to bear out that judgement all too clearly. Dynamic we were not.

My memories of the first couple of years are devoid of all colour. By and large we only met every four months or so and invariably chose days that were cold, miserable and grey. It was hardly a good time to be claiming that capitalism had outlived its historical usefulness. All over Europe a revitalised Social Democracy was coming to power, confident that it could manage the free market better than the Hard Right. The future seemed to belong to Tony Blair, Gerhard Schröder and Lionel Jospin. I confess that I never disliked Blairism as much as some of my comrades. To me it seemed like a sensible and well-meaning attempt to wean the country off some of Thatcherism's more austere dogmas, and there were plenty of occasions when I considered cutting my losses and going over to the Labour Party. The contrast between the dynamism of the government and the sclerosis of the Communist Party often struck me as demeaning. The Blairites were rescuing the welfare state, introducing the minimum wage and overhauling the constitution while we were pronouncing pointless anathemas

Britain (CPGB) was eventually dissolved in 1991, a few months after the failed coup that effectively brought the USSR to an end. The organisation I joined in 1997 was the Communist Party of Britain (CPB), one of several parties that claim to have 're-established' the communist tradition in Britain.

from the sidelines. For a long time I felt sure that my ties with British communism would dissolve at any minute. My second defection seemed imminent.

But then, in the mellow autumn of 1999 – as the world prepared to wash its hands of the twentieth century – the emotional weather began to change. Two things occurred which persuaded me that rejoining the Party had been the right thing to do. One was resoundingly public and the other entirely private. I can think of no better way of bringing this chronicle of ambivalence to an end than by describing both of them.

On the last day of November a meeting of the World Trade Organisation (WTO) opened in Seattle. Ordinarily it might have been assigned a two-minute segment about halfway through the news. That night it made headlines across the planet. Entirely out of the blue, wholly unpredicted even by those of us who thought we had our ears to the ground, Seattle played host to the biggest political riot in the Western world since 1968. The footage beggared belief. Thousands of gnarled anarchists, stroppy greens and surly trade unionists held the city to ransom for nearly three days, threatening at any moment to smash their way through the security barriers and give the besuited representatives of international capital a taste of rough proletarian justice. It was more a piece of high-energy theatre than an ordinary political demo. The protestors took care to ensure that every inch of the territory they occupied (the military metaphor is not inappropriate) resonated with their presence. Men and women carrying black flags and placards marched down the streets in menacing phalanxes, many of them wearing balaclavas or gas masks to conceal their identities from the Surveillance State. Canisters of thick black smoke sent apocalyptic clouds surging through the skies. Contingents of street musicians beat out tribal rhythms on African drums. It was not the kind of environment in which social order could be maintained for even a second. No one pretended that he had come in peace. Apoplectic young men hurled rocks, Molotov cocktails and other improvised missiles at the disbelieving riot police, suddenly impotent behind their shields and visors. The windows of McDonald's, Starbucks and other symbols of global free marketry were summarily smashed. A slogan on one of the banners summed things up: 'If humanity is to live, capitalism must die'.

I should have been appalled. Since the age of fifteen I'd been a prissy parliamentary socialist, utterly opposed to the idea that political progress required barricades, insurrections and broken bones. Yet the news from Seattle made the hair on the back of my neck stand to attention. I knew straightaway that the riots opened a new chapter in the struggle for human liberation. For nearly a decade the instincts of people everywhere had been ruthlessly reconfigured in the interests of global capital. Chastened by the collapse of socialism and powerless before the expansion of international markets, even the most disaffected among us had come to regard the dream of a new life as an embarrassing relic of mankind's collective adolescence. The great significance of Seattle was that it mocked our defeatism by *forcing us to feel differently*. I didn't believe for a moment that the *enragés* on the street had any answers to the world's problems, nor would I have wished to be governed by them for even a second. But that was hardly the point. Their function was not to provide a blueprint for a new society but to purify us with their rage. By calling down curses on an intolerable system – by screaming in our faces and imploring us to recognise that humanity deserved better than the clammy embrace of the status quo – they fertilised the emotional soil in which a more thoughtful form of politics could grow. They were, if you like, the storm before the calm. In *The Eighteenth Brumaire of Louis Napoleon* (1852), one of the books that affected me most deeply during my teens, Marx famously described the Revolution as a patient and indefatigable mole which burrows furiously underground before it can thrust its head triumphantly through the surface of the earth.[69] Seattle was the first sign that the mole's underground labours continued unabated.

69 See Karl Marx, *Surveys from Exile* (Harmondsworth: Pelican, 1973), p. 237.

The other memorable event occurred on the first Sunday in December, a week or so after Seattle had roused us from our slumbers. In the afternoon I attended a Branch meeting at which mince pies and glasses of sherry were handed out to mark the approach of Christmas. At one point, describing a conference on the environment he'd attended many years earlier, the Branch Secretary recalled an uninspiring conversation with the ecological guru Edward Goldsmith. 'The man was clearly mad', he said. 'As far as I could tell he wanted us all to become hunter gatherers again.' Retrieving a few crumbs of pastry from her jumper and popping them in her mouth, Linda immediately chimed in with one of what we used to call her 'more impoverished than thou' remarks. 'Listen', she barked. 'Some of us have never *stopped* being hunter gatherers.' Everyone laughed and we moved on to a slightly portentous discussion about 'Party work in the new century'.

At the end of the meeting I asked Linda what she'd meant by her remark. Strongly implying that I had no knowledge whatsoever of the dire conditions in which the poor are obliged to live, she told me that the unemployed have always had to avail themselves of the things that cities give out for free. 'It's not possible to stay alive if you only rely on the dole', or so she claimed in her most blustering manner. 'Those of us on the wrong side of the tracks have no choice but to scavenge in the street. Every week I tour the city and gratefully accept whatever it has to offer. In fact I'll be going out tonight for an hour. If you want to see a modern hunter gatherer in action, meet me outside the railway station at eleven o' clock'.

Normally I'd have done anything to get out of one of Linda's invitations, but there was something in what she said that intrigued me. Over the previous few months I'd become increasingly interested in the study of prehistory. According to the Marxist historians whose work I'd been reading, the age of the hunter gatherers was essentially one of 'primitive communism'.[70] In

70 I'd been especially impressed by V. Gordon Childe's *Man Makes Himself* (London: Watts, 1948 [1936]) and Jack Lindsay's *A Short History of Culture* (London: Gollancz, 1939). The most important account of primitive

the eternity of centuries between the emergence of *homo sapiens* and the first agricultural settlements, men and women had lived in classless societies, operated a vigorous tribal democracy and held all their property in common. That at least was the theory and I was more than willing to believe it. The thought that our ancestors had been free of the taint of class lent credence to the idea that the future could be classless too. As I thought of Linda roaming around the city in search of tasty morsels to eat, I began to envision her as a sort of latterday tribeswoman who had somehow preserved the communist instincts of a remote but inspiring age. The prospect of seeing her in action was too beguiling to resist. I told her I'd see her later.

By the time we met a strong wind had got up and large clouds were blowing ominously across the night sky. The expanse of neon-lit pavement in front of the railway station had never seemed so bleak. I tried to insulate myself against the cold by pulling my scarf up around my chin and burying my hands deep in the pockets of my overcoat. It was all to no avail: Every few minutes I had to make a conscious effort to stave off a shivering fit. Doing her best to control her straggly hair as it blew across her face, Linda took a few seconds to brief me about the mission that lay ahead. She explained that it was too late in the year to get a truly satisfying haul but that one place in particular would probably yield a 'cornucopia of delights'. It was unlike her to use such extravagant language and it seemed that the thought of adventure had temporarily quickened her blood. As we headed off down Alexandra Road, making good time past the darkened shell of the library where I'd first attended meetings of the SPGB, she told me to keep my eyes peeled for cigarette butts containing serviceable amounts of tobacco. Her own eyes scanned the road as alertly as those of an urban fox foraging for food. Almost immediately we found a discarded box of Benson and Hedges with a single unsmoked cigarette still nestling in it. Linda lit it straightaway and the smell of smoke on the city

communism in the Marxist tradition can be found in Frederick Engels's *The Origin of the Family, Private Property and the State* (1884).

streets took me back to a hundred adolescent afternoons, Julian exhaling clouds of cheap tobacco through his nose as we traipsed along talking of punk, the evils of Thatcherism and the promise of the revolution. It seemed like a good omen.

At the end of Alexandra Road we climbed one of the steep hills above the city and tried our luck in the unkempt gardens behind the towering Edwardian houses. Strictly speaking this wasn't theft: Most of the houses were occupied by tenants and no one ever ventured out the back. One of the gardens offered up a decent supply of fennel, which Linda stuffed into a large canvas bag slung across her shoulder. Another boasted an apple tree which still had three or four undistinguished specimens clinging to its branches, undefeated by the autumn winds. But that was all – otherwise the larder was bare. Linda didn't let the setback discourage her, consoling herself on the walk back down the hill with a vivid, enraptured and wildly exaggerated description of the rich pickings that awaited her in the spring. Then she shot me a significant look and tried to whet my appetite for the business still ahead of us with an image straight out of the Middle Ages: 'And now', she said, 'let me take you to the place where the steaks grow on the trees and the rivers flow with milk and honey'.

It turned out that Linda's sumptuary utopia, her personal version of the Land of Cockaigne, stretched for about five feet at the rear entrance of one of Swansea's most expensive hotels. To the uninitiated eye it looked like a ramshackle assemblage of cardboard boxes, rubbish bags and wheelie bins. Yet what Linda knew – and what most other members of Swansea's poor apparently did not know – was that every Sunday evening, in preparation for the week ahead, the kitchen staff threw out all the food that had technically passed its sell-by date. The abandoned riches were the stuff of a pauper's wet dream. Whole cheeses, cartons of milk, rashers of bacon, mounds of apples, pears and oranges, sherry trifles and enormous chocolate gateaux – there was enough to keep a family of twenty Falstaffs in roistering good spirits for at least a fortnight. Linda liberated every last crumb with ruthless efficiency. Instructing me to look inconspicuous while keeping an eye out for security guards, she identified what was still edible with a single sweeping glance and shovelled it into her bag with a practised hand. There was no hint of greed or rapacity on her face, simply undiluted pleasure at the thought of scoring a small victory over the system. 'You can't possibly eat all that yourself', I laughed. 'Of course not, boy', she replied. 'I keep a small amount for myself and give the rest to the poorer families on the estate'. It was one of those moments when one suddenly sees an old friend in an entirely new light. I had always regarded Linda as a dedicated activist, a formidable debater and a razor-sharp Marxist scholar but it had never occurred to me that she might be a benefactor of the oppressed. How wrong I was. The old trouper had been Robin Hood all along.

Our night's labours were over. Linda wished me goodnight and headed off down Alexandra Road towards her council flat, stooping slightly under the weight of all the food. There was nothing feigned about the feelings of affection and admiration which welled up inside me as I watched her go on her way. In some part of my mind I realised that it was absurd to regard her as a hunter gatherer *de nos jours*. I didn't need to be told that there was all the difference in the world between hunting bison on the Serengeti and pinching cheese, gateau and trifle from an expensive hotel. And yet, in spite of all my historical scruples, I somehow knew that from now on I would always think of her as a missing link between the upper Palaeolithic and the end times of late capitalism. With her gift for locating sources of free food in a hostile city and her uncompromising insistence that the booty be shared out equally among her kinsfolk, she gestured towards a past in which no one thought himself better than anyone else and everyone said 'this is ours' but never 'this is mine'. In reminding us that communism had once been the natural order of things, she incarnated the hope that one day – at a much higher level of technology and culture and at a much lower level of superstition – we could do it all again. These were heady thoughts for a cold night in December.

Linda didn't bother to wave before she turned left at the end of the road and disappeared from view. She probably didn't realise that I'd been watching her. Suddenly alone on one of Swansea's less salubrious thoroughfares, I turned swiftly on my heels and strode off towards the car park. In the morning I was due to give a lecture at the university and in the meantime I needed all the sleep I could get.

A new millennium was about to begin.

AFTERWORD

This book ends in December 1999 because that was the month in which history restarted. The Seattle insurgency settled the question of whether the left had a future as well as a past. No one who watched the footage of youthful *enragés* clashing with bewildered riot police could have any doubt that rumours of capitalism's outright victory had been greatly exaggerated. Across Europe and North America the culture of the left suddenly seemed more buoyant. Activists everywhere breathed a sigh of relief and settled to the work of building the resistance. Fukuyama's claim that history had run aground on the barren shores of liberal capitalism now stood revealed for what it was: an empty boast from the dog days of a dying century. The long march towards human liberation was underway again.

No doubt there were many people in that post-Seattle dawn who believed that the Marxist parties could continue as they had before, untroubled by the need to question their ideas, their strategies or their forms of organisation. Yet for a few years the atmosphere on the left was anything but dogmatic. Although the Communist Party, the SWP and all the other Marxist sects seemed much the same in 2001 as they had ten years earlier, many of us had the sense that the old ways were liquefying in front of our eyes. We had no clear idea of what should come next but we had no doubt that the socialist project would soon be completely overhauled. This expectation of imminent change ran from the bottom of the movement to the top. It shaped the mental reflexes of ordinary activists as much as those of high-falutin academics. The red professors in their fifties and sixties united with placard-wielding teenagers to proclaim the coming of a new dawn.

It was hardly surprising that words like 'democracy', 'freedom' and 'human rights' should have featured so prominently in the debates of those years. Looking back over the harrowing course of the twentieth century, even the most purblind militant was forced to acknowledge that the Marxist left had done more to murder the working class than to liberate it. It was clear that we would make no progress at all until the last residues of Stalinism were expunged. What was remarkable about the early noughties was that so many people seemed willing to come clean about their own democratic failures. Instead of claiming that contempt for freedom was someone else's problem – instead of insisting that Stalinism ran rampant elsewhere but that our own particular party or sect was free of it – we began to accept that our most encrusted principles and practices were often far less democratic than we had sometimes supposed. It was a time when one could question the entire political culture associated with the October Revolution without being denounced as a fifth columnist. Some adventurous souls suggested that our commitment to Leninist forms of organisation was increasingly passé – perhaps, or so it was said, there was a direct line of descent between *What is to be Done?* and the gulags. Others went so far as to say that the Bolshevik project had been compromised from the start, rendered incipiently tyrannical by its belief that socialist governments could legitimately withhold democratic rights from the bourgeoisie. Heresy seared through the air.

As someone whose involvement in the Leninist left had always been complicated by an implacable and perhaps simple-minded faith in democracy, I welcomed the new mood of liberal openness. It seemed to me that it wasn't enough simply to change our own structures. It was also necessary to incorporate the demand for democratic reforms into our day-to-day campaigns. Some of my more historically aware comrades accused me of harking back to Karl Kautsky and the ideological obsessions of the Second International, but in fact I derived my inspiration from a much more contemporary source.The writers who really gripped me at that time had all been associated with the Revolutionary Communist Party (RCP), a sort of post-Trotskyist academy of political provocation which had dissolved itself in 1998. Their doyen was the Anglo-Hungarian academic Frank Furedi – a much-respected lecturer at the university in which I took my first degree – but their message was disseminated with equal flair by the likes of Mick Hume, Brendan O'Neill and Claire Fox. The point about Furedi and his co-thinkers was that their work had taken a startling left-libertarian turn in the mid-1990s.[71] Surveying the affluent societies of the West as the twentieth century drew to a close, they argued that the politics of anti-capitalism had been derailed by a collective failure of nerve. Too many aspects of modern Western culture undermined our sense of what human beings could do by traducing their greatest achievements and eroding their most precious freedoms. The demonisation of science and industry by witless greens, the assault on free speech by politically correct bigots, the increased interference in people's personal lives by overbearing and officious governments – all these things and others demoralised the individual and convinced her that fundamental change was impossible to achieve. The only solution was to launch an uncompromising offensive against all the life-denying nonsense which sapped the West's confidence. Before we could think about establishing a new society – before we could sweep capitalism into the dustbin of history for once and for all – we had to restore people's faith in themselves by pressing home the case for science, reason, individual liberty and free speech. The commitment to democratic values was no peripheral part of the socialist project, or so Furedi and his followers averred. Socialism simply could not survive without it.

I don't think many people on the left were influenced by

71 The RCP outlined its left-libertarian turn in *The Point is to Change It: A Manifesto for a World Fit for People* (London: Junius Publications, 1996). Furedi, Hume and its other leading thinkers honed their ideas in the monthly magazine *Living Marxism*, easily the best British Marxist journal of the 1990s. Known as *LM* from 1998 onwards, the magazine was put out of business in 2000 after losing a spiteful libel case brought by ITN.

the RCP's libertarian heresies, but to me they pointed the way with irresistible force to the post-Leninist future. That's why the next twist in the plot was so distressing. Just as our quest for a new political culture seemed on the verge of bearing fruit, the democratic enthusiasms of the early noughties began to fade. Towards the end of 2001 there was a noticeable hardening of the atmosphere in the Marxist sects. Suddenly our cautious rapprochement with the gods of reason, free speech and personal autonomy seemed like a luxury we could not afford. Bewildered by the new and cataclysmic phase of globalisation brought about by the events of 9/11, Marxists everywhere behaved as if liberal scruples were an unpardonable distraction from the task of resisting imperialist wars. At about this time I commended the work of Frank Furedi in a throwaway line in an article I wrote for a communist newspaper. The sentence was edited out.

It wasn't simply that the invasions of Afghanistan and Iraq convinced the left that there were more pressing things to do than debate its own values. The entire political conjuncture seemed to be conspiring to discredit the democratic idea. When the USA, Britain and their allies sent their armies to the Middle East, they justified their actions by invoking the tenets of neoconservatism. They claimed that their objective was not merely to topple tyrannical governments and defeat terrorism but also to establish functioning democracies. This was supposed to drain the Islamic countries of their sectarian hatreds and make them more sympathetic towards the West. The manifest failure of the Western armies to realise the neoconservative dream – the rapid descent of Kandahar, Baghdad or Fallujah into bloodstained hellholes – made it so much easier for the left to revive the tired old idea that liberal democracy was nothing more than a fraudulent cover for capitalist interests. The situation got worse when we insisted on treating our enemy's enemy as our friend. Startled by the ease with which the Taliban and the Iraqi Resistance inflicted losses on the Western armies, many people on the left came to see them as anti-imperialist heroes rather than brutal exponents of religious fascism at its most depraved. There was a time not so long ago when the British left's most prominent spokesman was George Galloway, a man whose drooling sycophancy towards Middle Eastern terrorists, dictators and spivs has become proverbial. It was the only time in my life when my habitual unease about my own side curdled into shame.

It would be nice to report that the left's descent into Middle Eastern madness has passed into history. And to a certain extent it has. In 2008 the world lurched into the biggest capitalist crisis since the 1930s. Anti-imperialist heroics suddenly seemed less important than the need to protect ordinary people against the worst effects of austerity. As the left tried to come to terms with the implosion of the banks, the massive rise in unemployment and the imposition of what we always liked to call 'vicious cuts', it began once again to appreciate the virtues of openness and free discussion. Recognising that the forces opposing austerity were painfully scattered and thin on the ground, it set about establishing local anti-cuts movements which cheerfully embraced anyone who was willing to lend a hand. The result has been the slow emergence of a new public sphere of the left. Communists, anarchists, Trotskyists and ageing Bennites have gathered in the same draughty rooms and patiently traded ideas. Voices have been raised but rarely to fever pitch. Those of us for whom hope still triumphs over experience – those of us so inured to defeat that we no longer feel the weight of the enemy's blows – cherish the idea that these fragile new movements might one day blossom into a genuinely unified, genuinely democratic party of the left. The chances are against it. The old sectarian habits and the sneeringly illiberal impulses are still there. But we can only start from where we are.

The current political situation is nothing if not paradoxical. International capitalism is at a singularly low ebb but the left seems incapable of challenging it. After thirty years as a Marxist foot soldier I'm inclined to shy away from the left's more overheated rhetoric, but even now I'm prepared to stifle my embarrassment and affirm that socialism is still what we in

Wales used to call 'the hope of the world'. The future is as open-ended as it ever was. History has not yet run its course. It is still possible to spurn the dust and win the prize.

ACKNOWLEDGEMENTS

I am grateful to Mala Jagmohan and Sara Robb for encouraging me to write this book and to Tony Zurbrugg and Adrian Howe at Merlin for choosing to publish it. I am also grateful to Noorul Hasan, Lyndon White and Bob Davies for their comments on the manuscript. Edward Parr helped me navigate my way through the world of the hard left when he and I were *soi-disant* revolutionaries in our mid-teens. I shall always associate him with what Eric Hobsbawm once called the 'miraculous revelations of youth'. Howard Moss of Swansea University wrote a very flattering reader's report on the book and generously recommended it for publication. Howard is one of the Welsh left's most distinctive, humane and rational voices and embodies all the best qualities of the Socialist Party of Great Britain, an organisation of which he has been a leading member since the 1970s. I owe a big debt to Carolyn Brown for her advice, her support and her adamantine insistence that certain contentious passages should not be excised. Carolyn is an unfailing source of insight and *joie de vivre*: I thank her for everything.

My biggest debt of all is to Daisy Hasan. It was Daisy who suggested that I write this book and she who created the circumstances in which it was possible to do so. Her generosity, her superhuman tolerance and her immense literary and intellectual gifts never cease to amaze me. *Notes from the End of History* is dedicated to her.

INDEX

Also published by The Merlin Press

Philip Bounds
British Communism and the Politics of Literature, 1928-1939

In the 1930s, writers associated with the Communist Party of Great Britain set out to transform English culture. Creating a substantial body of Marxist literary criticism, and drawing on ideas from their own cultural traditions and from the Soviet Union, critics such as Christopher Caudwell, Alick West and Ralph Fox showed how Marxism could play a major role in analysing literature and its place in society.

This book is the first full-length study of the British communist critics of the Thirties. Seeking to relate Marxist literary criticism to the broader history of the communist movement, it shows how the work of the leading critics both reflected and subverted the left-wing orthodoxies of the day.

"This is an excellent study of a fascinating phenomenon ... Bounds skilfully evokes the political and cultural context in which these theorists wrote, and brings out the distinctive contribution of each of them. Solid research, sharp analysis and good writing make this book a pleasure to read." ? Professor Vincent Geoghegan, Queen's University, Belfast and author of *Utopianism and Marxism*

'a very welcome contribution.' *North West Labour History*

'should be read by all students of Marxism and literature.' *Socialist Review*

'the fact that it's not written in opaque academese makes it accessible to the general reader and as such it is a valuable and welcome contribution to the study of the communist party and its historical contribution to cultural life in Britain.' *Morning Star*

ISBN. 978-0-85036-594-8 328 pages paperback